Amaryllis

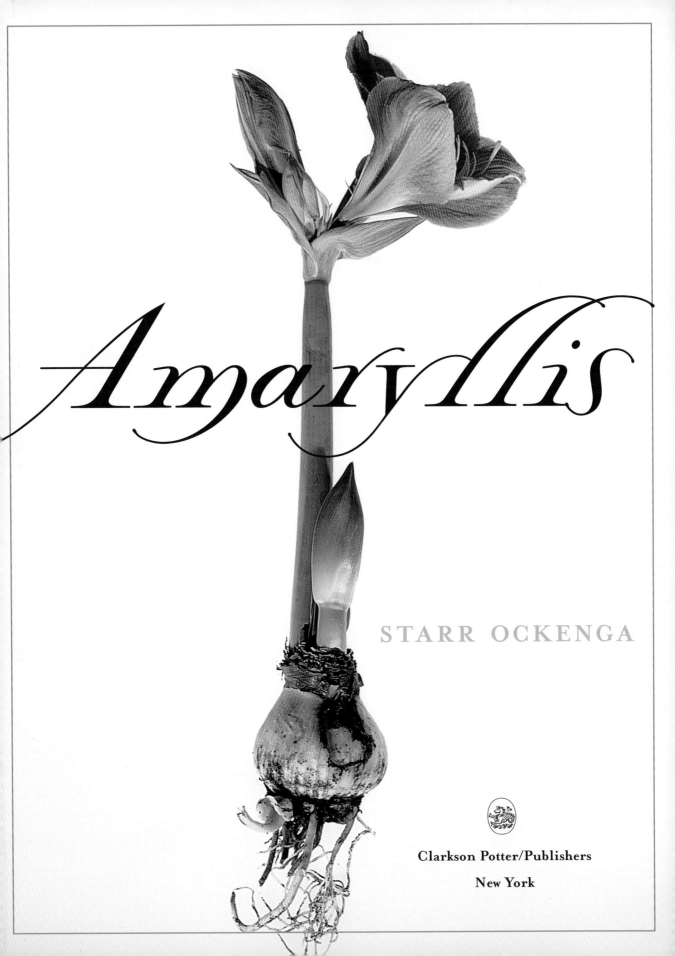

Amaryllis

STARR OCKENGA

Clarkson Potter/Publishers

New York

Also by Starr Ockenga
Earth on Her Hands: The American Woman in Her Garden
Eden on Their Minds: American Gardeners with Bold Visions

Published by Clarkson Potter/Publishers, New York, New York.
Member of the Crown Publishing Group, a division of Random House, Inc.
www.randomhouse.com

CLARKSON N. POTTER is a trademark and POTTER and
colophon are registered trademarks of Random House, Inc.

Printed in China

DESIGN BY YOLANDA CUOMO, NYC
Design associate, Kristi Norgaard

Library of Congress Cataloging-in-Publication Data
Ockenga, Starr.
Amaryllis / written and photographed by Starr Ockenga.—1st ed.
p.   cm.
Includes bibliographical references (p.).
1. Hippeastrum.   2. Amaryllis (Genus)   I. Title.
SB413.A5 O34   2002
635.9'3434—dc21   2001059322

ISBN 0-609-60881-9

10   9   8   7   6   5   4   3   2   1

First Edition

Previous pages: left, 'Blushing Bride'; right, 'Summertime'.
Opposite: 'Ludwig Dazzler'.

For Robin, my son
The light of my life, each day and forever

CHAPTER *1*

amaryllis through the centuries

A History

of Hippeastrum...*17*

CHAPTER *2*

making magic

Amaryllis

Care

and

Cultivation...34

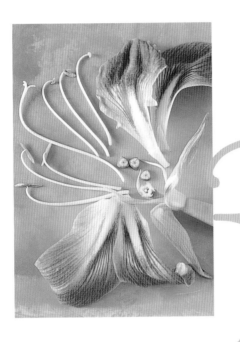

CHAPTER 3

CHAPTER 4

INTRODUCTION

in a quiet light

This book is a personal journal, the story of the winter I grew and photographed a court of amaryllis royalty. Over the season its number reached three hundred and fifty plants, representing more than ninety varieties.

I had recently built a studio with an attached greenhouse in the middle of my garden. The little fenced complex, which sits on a remote slope facing the Catskills, is my modern interpretation of a medieval cloister. This peaceful environment, the realization of a lifelong dream, is where I retreat to do my work. Even when my gardens sleep and the cold winds tear south from Canada and across our hilltop, the greenhouse is my haven, allowing me to keep my hands in the earth when the ground around the building freezes solid.

Upon moving into the new greenhouse I succumbed to the northern gardener's tropical fever: the lure of exotic plants. I bought clivias and freesias, orchids and veltheimias. Into the mix I added several amaryllis hybrids and was instantly smitten. Before long I had turned my back on the rest and focused on the amaryllis, thrilling to their architectural stature, brilliant wardrobes, and enigmatic personalities.

I concentrated on Dutch and African hybrids, those magnificent specimens now readily available from catalogs, garden centers, and flower shops. Working with these flowers day after day, I came to know each by name and to think of them as individuals or characters in a play. 'Basuto' makes a powerful entrance, clad in iridescent, velvety red, one of the first Africans to bloom. 'Milady', petite and draped in the deep raspberry of a diva's dressing gown, belongs in a boudoir scene, while 'Blushing Bride' tilts her ruffled pink head with shy modesty. The fragile surface of lightly fragrant double 'Jewel' suggests a mythic virgin's pearly flesh, and 'Rozetta' is a rotund little crowd pleaser, with her rosy, frill-framed face. 'Jaguar', brilliantly striped in skin of brownish red, is a cat, and 'Giraffe', with long neck and delicate head swaying back and forth in the currents of the greenhouse fan,

'Picotee' was one of my stars. Erect with regal bearing, it flowered in pure white with crimson tracing at its petals' edges.

9

Throughout the winter,
my greenhouse became an
exotic world, albeit with a
concentration on one plant:
the amaryllis.

maintains its namesake's awkward grace. In my green-house theater, outfitted with simple stage sets and painted backdrops, some of my "actors" stepped forward to assume the leads, and others appeared content to remain in the chorus. All, however, seemed photogenic.

Besides being seduced by the plant as a subject for my camera, I also became curious about its history. What does the name *amaryllis* mean? In what tropical paradise did its ancestors originate? What plant hunters', botanists', and breeders' names are linked to it? Where and how is the bulb propagated today? How is its anatomy defined? What is the plant's range of color and form? What is the best way to grow it, and under what conditions can it be rejuvenated year after year? I launched on a quest for answers, becoming more intrigued with each new discovery.

Without visualizing exactly how I would house all these plants—ultimately, they crowded every greenhouse bench and six permanent and makeshift tables through-out my studio—I placed orders with a half dozen sup-pliers. Restraint was not part of the equation; I wanted to try every variety I could find. While the glossary in this book is not intended to be definitive, because new culti-vars are added each season, it does represent the enormous range of amaryllis hybrids available in today's market.

From the arrival of the first carton of bulbs in mid-October through the end of May, when the last flowers faded, I kept a log. I recorded the date I planted each bulb and when it came into flower; the form, size, and scale of the plant and its blossoms; and myriad other details about the growing process. Simultaneously, I hunted for articles and books, especially historical sources, on the subject.

I photographed every morning, recording each plant in all stages, from highly textured bulb to audacious flower, from shriveled blossom to ripe seed head. Looking

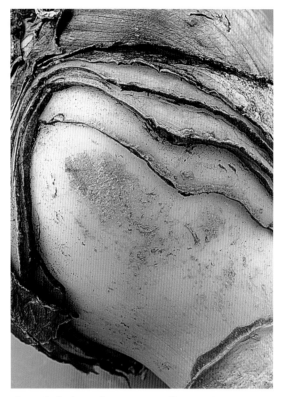

through the lens of a camera at a flower is intoxicating, particularly close up as it morphs from reality into abstraction. I have always believed that the more narrow the parameters of a project, the farther the adventure may take me. When squeezing my ideas through the neck of a funnel, suddenly the world opens to new possibilities. I determined that I would confront this one flower, the amaryllis, and use only natural light. Thus, over a six-month growing period I focused my work within two constraints and their infinite variables. Just to pull the rope a little tighter, I also confined myself to one camera (a Mamiya 645), one lens (a slightly telephoto 120 Macro), and one film type (Kodak SW100).

I documented the way the flowers grew, respecting their different habits. Later I augmented their number with a few varieties I found in New York City's flower district, tenderly transporting the fragile blossoms north in my Jeep. While snow swirled outside the glass walls, my arcadia glowed in a rainbow of reds, oranges, pinks, and creamy whites.

Throughout the months of making portraits, each variety's qualities remained distinctive. Still, I could not help becoming partial. Often the ones that captured my affections showed quirky traits. 'Charmeur', in a gesture of attention-grabbing, sent a flower out the side of the bulb with almost no stem. 'Ludwig Dazzler' seemed to perform a jazz troupe's free-form gyrations in the opening of its flowers. The abstract landscapes discovered in the close-up views of 'Lilac Wonder', 'Hermitage', 'Bold Leader', 'Summertime', 'Minerva', and 'Ambiance' took my breath away.

As they came in and out of bloom, the changing displays of amaryllis enlivened the rooms of our home for months. One always sat beside my reading chair, like a bright companion, and a cluster of reds—'Noel', 'Bold Leader', and 'Merry Christmas'—arranged in the entry hall provided a holiday welcome. I used them to decorate our dinner table, placing a single blossom of the salmon- and white-striped 'Andes' in front of each plate. I gave them to friends as gifts so often, my nickname was "the Amaryllis Lady."

nd so, the amaryllis and

On the first of May, the gardens beckoned, and I stopped making photographs. I moved the amaryllis pots to the greenhouse courtyard, where their newly grown foliage could mature and they could spend the spring and summer restoring their strength for next year's return.

Nature, the temptress, is unpredictable. A plant that behaved one way for me may do something entirely different for you. Those surprises, those unknowns, are the siren's song that calls us to the garden—and propels us to attempt feats we have not tried before.

I kept company oil through the winter

amaryllis
through the centuries

A HISTORY OF HIPPEASTRUM

Amaryllis: elegant, sensual, and mysterious. A tender tropical plant, the amaryllis bursts into magisterial flower from an oversized bulb.

The virtues of amaryllis are many. To begin with, it is easy to grow. No coddling the first year is necessary, and it does not demand a faux winter in the refrigerator, as do crocus, hyacinth, and tulip. When you purchase your dynamo bulb, whether from the local garden center or from a mail-order nursery, it contains all the resources, energy, and determination to flower—almost no matter what you do. The bulb farm will have pushed, or "forced," your bulb into a state of readiness. The flower bud already resides inside its round belly. All you have to do is give it light and a little water; it is cued to perform.

No wonder, then, that this illustrious bulb has had a remarkable, if sometimes elusive, history.

According to the classical poets Theocritus, Ovid, and Virgil, Amaryllis was a virginal nymph, timid and shy but with a spine of steel. She fell deliriously in love with Alteo, an icy-hearted shepherd reputed to be as handsome as Apollo and as strong as Hercules, and determined that she would be true only to him, no matter what the consequences. Indifferent to her charms, Alteo claimed his only desire was that a new flower be brought to him, a flower that had never before existed in the world. Amaryllis consulted the Oracle at Delphi and was instructed to pierce her heart with a golden arrow at Alteo's door. This she did, dressed in maiden's white, for thirty consecutive nights, dripping blood all the while. The shepherd finally opened his door to discover a flower with crimson petals, which had sprung from the blood of Amaryllis's heart.

Amaryllis, whether female or flower, has been lauded by later poets as well. In his 1637 elegy to a drowned classmate, Lycidas, Milton wrote seductively of being tempted "to sport with Amaryllis in the shade."

Artists and photographers, too, have found inspiration in the flower. Pierre-

In my greenhouse the amaryllis is the reigning monarch of winter flowering plants.

A

fter a walk through the streets

of Edinburgh in 1855, Tennyson recalled "Here and there, on sandy beaches milky-bell'd amaryllis blew" in his poem "The Daisy."

Joseph Redouté made several meticulously detailed paintings of the amaryllis for Joséphine Bonaparte, suggesting that the empress favored the plant. The German entomologist and fine botanical artist Maria Sibylla Merian, who traveled to South America to paint indigenous moths and butterflies, included a painting of an amaryllis in *Metamorphosis Insectorum Surinamensium.* More recently, numerous Americans, from the Pennsylvania watercolorist Charles Demuth to the West Coast photographer Imogen Cunningham, both of whom made a specialty of rendering flowers closely viewed, celebrated the amaryllis.

Victorian volumes devoted to decoding the language of flowers attribute to the amaryllis characteristics ranging from haughtiness, pride, and determination to timidity and shyness. In her *Flora's Dictionary* (1829) Mrs. Elizabeth W. Wirt, credited with assembling the first floral dictionary in America, gave the meaning as "Splendid Beauty." A name with such romantic connotations, even contradictions, seems fitting for the queen of all bulbs.

However, the bulb we call amaryllis is not technically an amaryllis at all. Its taxonomy, while charming, is confusing and demands clarification. The actual genus *Amaryllis* contains only two species, *A. belladonna,* commonly known as the cape belladonna lily, and *A. paradisicola;* both come from the Cape Province of South Africa. Apparently, *A. belladonna*'s species name is an incorrect reference to a product favored by Renaissance women. Called belladonna, Italian for "beautiful woman," it is actually an extract from the

deadly nightshade plant, *Atropha belladonna,* rather than from an amaryllis; when used in eyedrop form it dilated the pupils and made them appear to sparkle. The Greek word *amarysso* or *amarussein,* from which "amaryllis" derives, means to sparkle, twinkle, scintillate, or shine. By that circuitous route "amaryllis" became synonymous with female beauty. But do not confuse our hybrids—which have passed through several name changes—with the true amaryllis, *A. belladonna,* a late-summer flowering bulb often grown in masses in southern California gardens.

One of the first mentions of the species in botanical literature is by Dr. Paul Hermann in *Paradisus Batavus* in 1698. A Dutch scientist, Hermann described a plant sent to him from the New World tropics for identification in 1689 as "Lilium americanum puniceo flore Bella Donna dictum" (the American lily with scarlet flowers called Belladonna).

In his plant classification treatise of 1700, *Eléments de botanique,* French botanist Joseph Pitton de Tournefort defined twenty-one species of bulbs with funnel-shaped flowers borne in umbel-shaped clusters at the top of a leafless stalk as *Lilio-Narcissus.* Carolus Linnaeus accepted de Tournefort's classification of the *Lilio-Narcissus* genus, first listing five species in *Hortus Cliffortianus* in 1737, then later encompassing nine in his 1753 *Species Planatarum.* Subsequently, Linnaeus, in creating the binomial system of plant classification—the system adhered to today by plant scientists throughout the world via the *International Code of Botanical Nomenclature*—eschewed hyphenated generic plant names. In homage to the beautiful nymph, Linnaeus renamed the group *Amaryllis,* the name that persists to this day.

An unfurling 'Angelique' flower bud reveals its distinctive veining on the outside of the petals.

The Honorable Reverend William Herbert, a British scientist and later dean of Manchester was a leading authority on the amaryllis of his era. He segregated some amaryllis into a new genus, which he called *Hippeastrum,* publishing the name change in his book *Amaryllidaceae* in 1837. Today *Hippeastrum* (hip-ee-**ay**-strum) remains the correct genus name for cultivated amaryllis hybrids.

Etymologically, the name is a combination of *hippos,* Greek for horse, or *hippeus,* rider, and *astron,* star, which loosely translated means the horseman's star, sometimes elevated to the more aristocratic knight's star lily. It is easy to see the reason for "star," for in many open amaryllis flowers a distinct star, often stark white against pink, red, or orange, marks the petals and the shape of the flowers. With a little imagination, the flower bud in progressive stages of opening can suggest the head of a horse. Early sources say *Hippeastrum puniceum* (also known as *H. equestre*), one of the first species to arrive in Europe, had a reddish-purple inflorescence. A reference in the English *Botanical Magazine* of 1795 declares that from particular angles, "The spatha is composed of two leaves, which standing up at

a certain period of the plants [*sic*] flowering like ears give to the whole flower a fancied resemblance to a horse's head."

The horticultural public, however, has failed to embrace the new name, and *Hippeastrum* hybrids still retain the common name amaryllis. Today the genus—in the Amaryllidaceae family—includes over fifty species, from which hundreds of cultivars have been bred.

History is murky as to when the amaryllis was discovered in South America. The species hail from the Andes Mountains of Chile, Peru, and Bolivia as well as from Brazil, Argentina, and Venezuela and as far north as Mexico and the West Indes. *H. puniceum, H. reginae, H. striatum, H. reticulatum,* and *H. vittatum,* probably in that order, were brought to Europe in the latter half of the seventeenth century, and additional species continued to be introduced as they were found. One account tells of Eduard Friedrich Poeppig, a young physician from Leipzig who journeyed to Peru on a plant hunting expedition in 1828, becoming so overcome with excitement at discovering the flower he purportedly shouted in triumph. Amaryllis had certainly reached North America by 1811, when Thomas Jefferson wrote to Bernard McMahon, the pioneering Philadelphia seedsman, of enjoying the "fine tulips, hyacinths, tuberoses & Amaryllis you formerly sent me." An 1889 Young and Elliott's catalog, complete with enticing drawings, lists five varieties, both species and hybrid, for the American consumer.

Parental origins of the *Hippeastrum* hybrids are obscure because they have been subjected to centuries of intensive breeding. The scarlet-petaled *H. reginae,* a native of the Peruvian Andes, was cultivated commercially in the early eighteenth century. Many of the modern hybrids derive

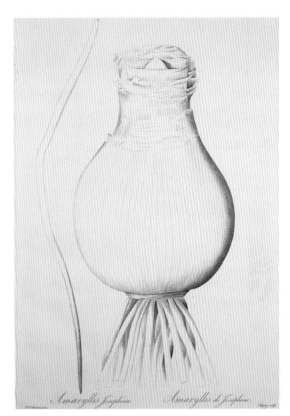

Amaryllis Josephine.   *Amaryllis de Josephine.*

from the profuse-flowered Brazilian *H. vittanum,* which was crossed with *H. reginae* in 1799 by Arthur Johnson, an English clock- and watchmaker; hence the first hybrid—*H. × johnsonii*—and, incidentally, one of the most cold-hardy hybrids even today. This variety, also called St. Joseph's lily, has bright red tepals, or petal-like parts, each featuring a central white stripe.

Over the next century and a half, particularly as more South American species arrived in Europe, breeders created hundreds of hybrids. A leading firm in Bristol, England, was Garroway & Company, where in 1835 *H. aulicum* var. *platypetalum* was crossed with *H. psittacinum* to create a much larger, open-faced flower, the hybrid *H. × acramannii.* Dutch breeders E. H. Krelage & Son listed 350 varieties in their 1863 catalog. Nonprofessional gardeners such as Louis van Houtte of Belgium produced green-throated hybrids that were used to further advance hybridization.

Two strains—*reginae* and *leopardii*—dominated the next period of breeding. The colorful *reginae* strain was developed by Dutch breeder Jan de Graaff and his two sons in the middle of the nineteenth century. They crossed *H. vittatum* and *H. striatum* with *H. psittacinum* and then with some of the European hybrids to net flowers with an extended palette of color, though they are small by today's standards. In 1865, two new South American species, *H. leopoldii* and *H. pardinum,* were discovered by intrepid plant hunter Richard William Pearce (who unfortunately died in 1867 at the age of twenty-nine from yellow fever contracted while in Panama). *H. leopoldii,* with its rounded tepals bent back to form large flat blooms, offered new breeding material. During the last quarter of the nineteenth century, growers, particularly the noteworthy James Veitch & Son of

Chelsea, England, experimented with crossing *H. leopardii* and *H. pardinum,* a species with a minutely dotted flower, with some of the de Graaff hybrids, thereby creating immense open flowers with short tepal tubes.

Most hybrids cultivated at that time produced only two flowers; breeders next sought to achieve four to six flowers per umbel. A cross of the eight-inch *H. leopoldii* with the de Graaff 'Empress of India' produced the desired results of multiple flowers, as well as dynamically larger size. Another advance was the first pure white *leopoldii* hybrid, produced in 1904 by C. R. Fielder, an estate gardener in North Mimms Park, England. Hybridization with other strains—*reginae, vittata,* and *reticulata*—produced flowers that were smaller but had a range of brilliant color from pink to deep vermilion.

During the mid to late nineteenth century, American growers—from California to Florida, from Illinois to Texas—began experimenting, particularly with *Hippeastrum × johnsonii* and some of the *vittata* hybrids. H. Pfister, head gardener at the White House for thirty years, worked with the van Houtte strain, *H. psittacinum,* and *leopoldii* hybrids. He named a rosy-red clone

Charles Demuth, American, 1883–1935. *Amaryllis*, c. 1923. Watercolor, 44.5 × 30 cm., courtesy The Cleveland Museum of Art, 2001, Hinman B. Hurlbut Collection. Opposite: 'Jaguar'.

'Mrs. Cleveland' for the president's wife and immortalized the president's daughters with 'Ruth', 'Marion', and 'Esther'.

From the 1890s through the 1920s, Dr. Henry Nehrling of Florida established one of this country's finest collections, boasting both species and hybrids. Theodore L. Mead's strain of giant hybrids, also grown in Florida, were started from the Nehrling superior germplasm. In the 1890s California too became a breeding center, beginning with a French nursery-man, George Compère, who initially brought his stock from France. Compère's efforts became the cornerstone for the work of the firm Howard & Smith in Montebello, where strains using Compère's crosses and *reginae* and *leopoldii* hybrids were bred. Even Luther Burbank of Santa Rosa, California, famed for his experimental work developing fine strains of fruit, bred amaryllis. He worked primarily with *H. johnsonii* and its predecessor *H. vittatum* to produce flowers that reached ten inches in size.

This vast assortment of hybrids graced the great con-

servatories and greenhouses of the wealthy for a century and a half. However, the fuel shortages of the two world wars brought to a close the era of heated glass structures; since the amaryllis is a tender bulb, much of the previous era's hybridization also ceased. Breeders like the renowned houses of Robert P. Ker, of Liverpool, England, and James Vetch and Sons, were forced to discontinue their work during World War I.

In 1919, Plant Quarantine 37 restricted the importation of amaryllis into the United States to a limited number of disease-free bulbs for propagation stock, which severely curtailed American amaryllis hybridization. Work did not stop, however. Through selective breeding, using English clones, the United States Department of Agriculture developed a new strain that ranged in color from blush pink through the reds to white with red stripes. The department held annual shows for the public from 1912 through 1939 (except in 1914–15).

The American Amaryllis Society was established in 1933. In *Herbertia,* its newsletter, which he edited at the time, Arno H. Nehrling, son of Dr. Henry Nehrling, noted Americans' growing interest in amaryllis. At one of the Department of Agriculture shows in the late 1930s, a "marvelous collection" of 1,200 bulbs drew close to 40,000 people. Through the society seeds and bulbs were disseminated from the Department of Agriculture's holdings to breeders throughout the country. Other avid horticulturists, such as Pierre S. Du Pont, who bred fine *reginae* and *leopoldii* hybrids at his estate, Longwood, in Pennsylvania, and Robert van Tress, horticulturist at Garfield Park Conservatory in Chicago and the creator of a vigorous red-orange strain, shared their results with other breeders.

The American Amaryllis Society immediately attracted an international membership.

Even in the midst of the Great Depression, economic belt-tightening did not extinguish America's love for plants. Dr. Hamilton P. Traub, one of the founders of the society and author of the comprehensive 1958 publication *The Amaryllis Manual,* wrote, "The number of persons interested in Amarylleae is undoubtedly great enough to support a thriving organization—not the largest but surely a high quality association." An important aspect of the society's activities was initiating the registry of new cultivars; in 1964 it published an updated, though not exhaustive, catalog of about 1,000 known hybrids. (The organization's seventy-five-year evolution has included name changes; currently it is the International Bulb Society, which reflects the membership's broader interest in "bulbous plants both rare and common.")

While hybridizing efforts flagged for several decades in the early and mid-twentieth century, it revived with gusto in the century's later years, particularly on the bulb farms of Holland. Traded through the great auction houses—the two largest being at Aalsmeer and Naaldwijk—or by contracts with growers, amaryllis are exported to various customers throughout the world. The Dutch, with innovative firms like G. C. van Meeuwen, Ludwig & Company, Kwekerij Den Oudendam, T. van Hermitage, and Penning Freesia, still lead the world in production for the bulb and cut flower markets. The flower industry is a backbone of the Netherlands' economy, bringing in over $3 billion a year. Bulbs are a substantial part of that market, with exports accounting for about three-quarters of a billion

While amaryllis with huge heads are beloved for their drama and presence, many collectors are seeking more subtle varieties, flowers with smaller faces, like 'Emerald'.

dollars, much of that coming from the United States, the world's leading bulb importer.

In Holland, commercially grown amaryllis, generally propagated from offsets or from twin-scaling, are primarily grown in large-scale greenhouse operations. Bulbs are planted from October to March and harvested by hand from July to October, when all their leaves are removed, chopped, and incorporated back in the planting beds. After harvesting, bulbs are quickly dried and cured. The old root system must remain viable.

The highly competitive flower industry is burgeoning in South Africa, and a number of American suppliers are increasingly dependent on that source for bulbs. Dutch bulb growers like Harry de Leeuw and Floor Barnhoorn, who migrated to South Africa in the 1940s, realized the virtues of *H. reginae,* which, while native to the Americas, had been introduced to Africa and was thriving there. A virus- and disease-resistant strain, it is easy to multiply from offsets; they began to cross it with their own hybrids to achieve new and spectacular flower colors. Since the 1970s the South African concentration has been on breeding cultivars with more scapes from smaller bulbs and larger flowers with extended life spans. Bulbs there are grown in outdoor fields; planting starts in July, and harvesting, all by hand, occurs in May.

While Holland and South Africa dominate in bulb production today, new hybrids are being developed in North America, Australia, Japan, India, Israel, and Brazil. Advancements being made in the United States are often the result of an individual breeder's efforts. For example, Charles "Dee" Cothran must be credited for 'Yellow Pioneer', a milestone in the quest for the elusive yellow amaryllis. (Sadly, by openly sharing with col-

Hippeastrum puniceum,
courtesy Herbarium, New York
Botanical Garden. Opposite:
the dried flower of 'Papilio'.
Overleaf: 'Star of Holland' bulb.

leagues, Cothan forfeited the right to proper acknowl-edgment or remuneration once the hybrid reached the commercial market.) From his work in raising over 40,000 *Hippeastrum* seedlings, the late Frederick G. Meyer, a former executive director of the International Bulb Society, made seventy cultivar selections that are being propagated to satisfy the demands of the cut flower, dry bulb, and forcing markets.

In breeding a new *Hippeastrum,* criteria for judgment include: flower color; flower shape and form; vase life for the cut flower market; the number of days from plant-ing to flowering; the number, height, and vigor of the scapes; the number of flowers per scape; and the bulb's root development and growth. In experimental pro-grams breeders are trying crosses with existing hybrids and species *Hippeastrum* or other genera of the family Amaryllidaceae with desirable characteristics—disease resistance, fragrance, cold-hardiness, or the still elusive yellow, purple, and blue colors. Of the hundreds that breeders cross-pollinate yearly, only a handful of hybrids make the cut. An amaryllis generally needs to reach a circumference of 26 to 28 centimeters before it will

bloom reliably; that takes two to four years. Then the labor-intensive process of bringing it to the commercial market begins, typically taking seven to nine years.

H. papilio, viewed as one of the most important twentieth-century introductions, is the focus of a breed-ing program run by Dr. Alan W. Meerow, which uses it as the primary species. Currently a research geneticist at the USDA's Subtropical Horticulture Research Station in Miami, Meerow has successfully introduced new cul-tivars that maintain the *papilio* characteristics of com-pact growth, evergreen foliage, and long-lasting flowers of unusual color range.

The United States Department of Agriculture imposes restrictions—standards based on regulations from the Agricultural Quality Act—on imported bulbs. All soil must be removed, and the bulbs must be washed and dried. Since that process shrinks the size of the bulbs slightly, the bulbs' measurements and resulting size classifications occur after the baths. Upon arrival in the States, bulbs are inspected by cus-toms and shipped to the importers' warehouses. Disseminated to mail order suppliers, they are then sorted, packaged, and shipped to the consumer—a complex but efficient journey.

When an amaryllis bulb arrives at your door, artfully wrapped and ready to grow, it carries a rich heritage, tales of intrepid plant explorers and dedicated breeders, of gigantic commercial endeavors and of individuals' care. Charles Barnhoorn, of the South African bulb company Hadeco, which has introduced numerous cul-tivars, reports that during the harvesting period alone, each bulb will pass through nine different sets of hands.

When I look at the splendid—sometimes even sublime—flower, I think, "It's all worth it."

When your amaryllis

bulb

arrives, you may discover that

it has been

individually and artfully

packaged

as if it were a fine

chocolate egg.

2

making magic

AMARYLLIS CARE AND CULTIVATION

One amaryllis lights up a room; a group of three or more creates a spectacular display. Yet for all the floral pyrotechnics they deliver, these blooms are simple to cultivate and will, given proper care, provide multiple years of pleasure. After completing its annual floral display, the plant demands food, in the form of fertilizer, to continue its cycle. Its foliage must be allowed to ripen and send fresh life back into the depleted bulb. Storing its newly gathered energy, it withdraws into its refuge, like a sleeping turtle, to take a seasonal snooze before once again bursting forth in glorious bloom.

Of course, it all begins with the bulb, and in choosing amaryllis bulbs it is wise to heed the old adage "Buy good, get good." Mail-order suppliers generally offer a wider selection of varieties than local garden centers. They try to send their bulbs to their customers as soon as they arrive in the warehouses, whereas bulbs in garden centers may sit for long stretches of time, which can dry out their roots and stunt the flowers.

Catalogs arrive in late spring or early summer. It is amusing to read other amaryllis enthusiasts' effusive descriptions, ripe with words like *radiant, luminous, exotic, glistening, velvety, lipstick-bright, candy-stripe,* and *floriferous.* Allow yourself to be enticed; order when you receive the catalogs or, if you are using the Internet, as soon as the new list is posted on your supplier's Web site, because favored varieties sell out quickly. Do not worry about having a houseful of blooming amaryllis in August; the bulbs will be shipped to you in the fall; the exact time is calculated according to the zone of your zip code. Since I garden in Zone 5, my bulbs arrived in October and early November.

If you are purchasing from a local garden center, look carefully at what you are buying. Healthy bulbs are firm and dry. Reject any that feel squishy or have dark, wet spots on the surface, which may indicate disease or bulb rot. A small amount of mold may have grown on the outer layer of the bulb while in transit and the

Plant a half a dozen of 'Papilio' in one pot for an understated, but inordinately elegant, display.

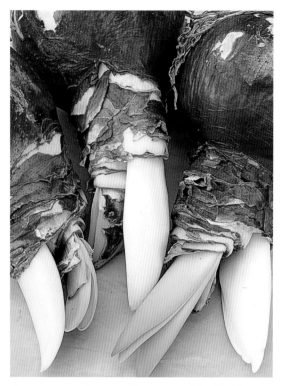

Three 'Rainbow' bulbs with spathes emerging.
Opposite: To test the theory that amaryllis bulbs arrive at
our doors with all the internal strength they need to
bloom, I set a couple of 'Ragtime' bulbs on a shelf under
the work counter in my greenhouse. I gave them no care;
while they received some light, they were neither
watered nor fertilized. They blossomed, making me feel
a little guilty for doubting their flower power.

Planting Amaryllis

The process of planting can be a Zen-like experience. Be sure you have your supplies in order and allow yourself the gift of time. I used two basic methods for planting my amaryllis. Most were planted in the traditional—and safest—manner, using a potting medium in terra-cotta pots. However, I experimented with a few, nestling their roots around a base of pebbles in glass containers half filled with water. Some of those water-grown amaryllis exceeded their potted siblings in size, and I enjoyed being able to see the entire bulb and its root development through the glass. However, growing an amaryllis bulb in water depletes its reserves; it could take several years for the plant to bloom again. If you decide to grow a water-grown amaryllis a second time, plant it in soil. Here are the basic guidelines for each method.

PLANTING AMARYLLIS BULBS IN POTS

1. Prepare a light, well-draining planting medium. The mix should be three parts premium-quality potting soil containing peat moss and vermiculite, such as Pro-Mix, and one part coarse sand. Amaryllis prefers a slightly acid soil with a pH between 6.0 and 6.5. The addition of sand improves drainage, a critical factor in success with amaryllis. Soggy soil is the enemy of amaryllis, as it is prone to bulb rot.

2. Amaryllis likes to be cozily pot bound. Choose a pot that is approximately an inch larger all around than your bulb. Be sure the pot has a drainage hole. I favor 6-inch, square, terra-cotta pots; the heft of the terra-cotta helps to counterbalance the size and weight of the flowers, and the depth allows space for root development. Do not plant in shallow bulb pans, as they do not

close quarters of storage; if you can rub it off, it has not hurt the bulb.

Examine bulbs purchased by mail immediately upon their arrival. The flower spathes' pointed tip—the "tongue"—may have pierced the top of the bulb; an inch or so of extension is acceptable. If the tip is visible, your bulb is jump-starting and should be planted immediately. Those light-starved tips will probably be pale green to almost white, which indicates that they have been in dark storage and have become chlorophyll deprived. Thanks to photosynthesis they will turn green within a day or two of being exposed to light. If extended white stems show or the bulb fails to meet your pinch test, call your supplier. Reputable firms will replace faulty bulbs.

In order to have a continuous season of bloom from the winter holidays to your garden's spring wake-up call, you may prefer to store some for later planting. If you stagger your bulb planting, store the bulbs in their bags in a cool, dry, frost-free location such as a closet, basement, or garage. Bring your bulbs out of their slumber a few at a time, planting them from October through February.

The bulb tag reads:

3
AMARYLLIS
SWEET SURRENDER
Double Royal Dutch Hybrid.
Pink and white.
30/32

9118

The Angelique plant marker reads:

Angelique Nº2.
Dutch single
Pink/White
Planted 10/25/0[?]

The bulb package label reads:

HYBRID AMARYLLIS
BESTSELLER

Clockwise from top left: 'Sweet Surrender' bulbs as they arrived from the distributor; potted bulbs, their planting mediums covered with moss, grass, and pebbles; soaking the bulbs' roots before planting gives them a head start; a newly potted 'Angelique' bulb reflects its planting date and bloom colors; the roots of an amaryllis grown in water are clearly visible; 'Calimero,' a miniature variety, is stem-tied to a stake for support; a bud and leaves emerging from a 'Bold Leader' bulb; self-watering pots like the one at right, shown planted with 'Rozetta,' keep bulbs from becoming waterlogged; 'Bestseller's' label foretells its showy pink blossoms.

provide enough room for the plant's roots. If you have used your pot before, be sure that you scrub it thoroughly with a diluted solution of household bleach—1 tablespoon of bleach to 1 quart of water—before reusing it.

3. Since terra-cotta is porous, a dry pot will act like a blotter and wick the water from your soil. Immerse your pot in a bucket of water until the pot stops hissing—at least five minutes. (Old garden manuals advise allowing pots to soak in water for weeks instead of minutes to allow them to absorb the maximum amount of water.)

4. Place squares of copper or plastic screen or broken pieces of terra-cotta in the bottom of the pots. The screen or chips and the gravel will prevent the planting medium from falling through the drainage hole or clogging it.

5. Examine your bulb and cut out and remove any dead, dried-out roots. Soak the fleshy roots, without immersing the bulb itself, in a shallow container filled with about an inch of tepid water for at least an hour, and up to several hours, if possible. This gives the roots a quick drink, which sends a signal to the bulb that it is time for action. In addition, the moistened roots, which may be a little brittle after their dormancy, will become pliable and easier to handle for planting.

6. Make a mound of soil in the bottom center of the pot about halfway up the sides. Gently arrange the moistened roots of the bulb over the mound of soil. Fill more soil around the bulb, making sure the top third of the bulb—its neck and shoulders—is clear of the soil. This shallow planting method prevents water from entering the crown of the bulb and rotting the flower bud.

7. Tuck the soil around the bulb firmly with your fingers to ensure that there are no air pockets. Gauge the placement of the bulb so that the top of the soil remains ½ inch below the rim of the pot, which will make watering more efficient. The pot may be decorated with a covering of stones or a layer of sheet or sphagnum moss. You can also plant violas or annual grasses, which can be clipped tidily, around the bulb, for a potted arrangement that looks like a miniature indoor garden.

8. If you are growing more than one variety, place a label with pertinent information at the side of the pot. I use white plastic labels available from greenhouse supply houses and a waterproof marker to record the variety's name, supplier, and planting date.

9. Water the soil around the bulb well with tepid water, being careful not to allow water to seep down between the layers of the bulb. Giving a good watering at the time you plant the bulb means that you may not have to water again until you see the flower bud pierce the top of the bulb.

10. Since these bulbs are native to the tropics, warmth and moisture will encourage them to break their dormancy. Place the pot in a bright room of 65 (night) to 75 (daytime) degrees. Amaryllis are sun worshipers during their flower-producing period, but once they are in bloom they should be moved to a less light location.

GROWING AMARYLLIS BULBS IN WATER

1. Choose a glass container that is an inch larger in diameter than the bulb. As an alternative, you may use an oversized bulb-forcing glass if it is large enough for the bulb to sit comfortably inside the rim.

2. Mound stones, such as marble chips or smooth river rock in the bottom of the container, about one-third of the way up the sides.

3. To make the roots of the bulb pliable, soak them as in step 5 above.

4. Set the bulb on the pyramid of stones and carefully spread the roots around the mound. Fill around the bulb with more stones to within ½ inch of the top of the container. Allow one-quarter to one-third of the bulb to be revealed above the stones.

Perhaps I was influenced by the power of suggestion, but it seemed that varieties lived up to their name—the seductive couple called 'Wedding Dance', right, or flapper-like air of 'Ragtime', opposite.

5. Add water to the base of the bulb only. Do not immerse the bulb in water.

6. Label your plant as in step 6 above.

7. Keep the water level at the base of the bulb. You can change the water periodically or add charcoal to keep it "sweet" and prevent algae from growing.

Ongoing Care

Amaryllis bulbs do not like to be overwatered. Water sparingly when they are first planted, until scape growth begins, keeping the soil moist, but never soggy. If in doubt, test the moisture level by pushing your finger down about an inch into the soil. If the soil feels cool and moist, do not add more water. Watering an amaryllis every three to five days, or even once a week, should be sufficient, depending on the heat and humidity in your home and the type of container used. Unlike terra-cotta and other unglazed pots, glazed containers will not lose moisture through their sides; thus, it will not be necessary to water them as frequently. Additionally, allowing the soil to dry out between watering helps prevent invasion by pests such as fungus gnats that make mischief in waterlogged soil.

Opinions about fertilizing during the flower-producing period are mixed. Some professionals advise a regular application of fertilizer. Others say it is unnecessary, that if a bulb sends up a flower shoot, you can be sure it contains all the fuel reserves it needs to produce its flowers. I followed this latter approach, did not fertilize, and had excellent results. If the plant produces foliage simultaneously with the flower stalk, you may fertilize with a half dilution of a 20-20-20 mixture. However, to prolong blooming, cease fertilization as soon as the flowers start to open.

An amaryllis often sends its flower stalks up before making foliage, particularly with the first flowering scape. Sometimes stalk and foliage emerge from the bulb simultaneously, particularly with the African hybrids, which concentrate their performance into a tighter time frame. Keep the foliage clean and free of dust by wiping the leaves with a damp cloth as needed. When the flower stalk, and possibly the foliage, elongates—which it does with seemingly magical rapidity—rotate the pot one quarter turn every day to keep the scapes from leaning toward the light.

Stake the stem, if necessary. Some long-stemmed, large-flowering varieties, like 'Apple Blossom' or 'Red Lion', become top-heavy and may capsize. Smaller doubles, like the delicate 'Snow White', have heads so full of ruffled petals that they cannot fight gravity, and the sheer weight of their headdresses drags them over. Even a prolific-blooming miniature like 'Calimero' may benefit from staking. Natural-colored bamboo stakes tied with raffia or hemp twine are the most unobtrusive support materials. Being careful not to damage the bulb, insert the stake close to it, and wiggle it down through

the roots until it touches the bottom of the pot. Attach the stake and stem with raffia or twine in a figure-eight formation at two points on the stem, as this is more stable than just one tie.

When the bulb flowers, move it to a cool place to extend the life of the blooms. Removing the anthers prevents pollination, which causes the flower, its reproductive work accomplished, to wither and die. (The procedure is more difficult with the doubles than with the singles.) When their anthers are removed, individual flowers last about a week. The remaining blossoms on that stalk open within a week to ten days. A few unfold simultaneously for a big bang display. Several of mine, like the delicate pink, double African 'Rozetta' or the prolific, velvety-red, Dutch single 'Floris Hecker', sent up three stems and remained in bloom for more than six weeks. My champion performer is the salmon- and

Left: 'Bold Leader'.

white-striped Dutch double, 'Andes', which first bloomed on Thanksgiving; its last flower withered on May Day.

Since most amaryllis blossom sequentially, they fade that way as well. Remove dead blooms. When all the flowers are gone, cut the stem 1 inch from the bulb's nose. Be sure to invert the cut stem quickly, as several drops of moisture are stored within the stem, which, if released on your upholstery or carpet, can cause a stain. Alternately, you may allow the flowerless scape to die back before cutting it off, which will send some food back into the bulb.

Preparing for the Next Season

You can encourage your amaryllis to perform for several years. However, once a bulb reaches a circumference of about 40 centimeters (about $15\frac{1}{2}$ inches), particularly one grown in a pot, it will not grow much larger. At that size the mother bulb may shrink in size and stop

CARING FOR CUT AMARYLLIS

From October through April many flower markets and florists import amaryllis from the Dutch, South African, and Israeli growers. Those varieties are often so new to the market that they have not yet reached the bulb suppliers. Since the flowers are fragile and subject to bruising, most are shipped in bud form.

Amaryllis stems are hollow and need to stay filled with water. Recut the stems on a 45-degree angle as soon as you bring them home and pour water into the stem with a small-necked watering can. Either plug the stem with cotton or hold your finger over the bottom of the stem while you place the flower in a vase.

Once in water and out of refrigeration, amaryllis will open and look fresh and vibrant. An arrangement of cut flowers—I favor a mass of one variety—makes a smashing bouquet, and if the flowers are kept in a cool location, they will last for a week or two.

'White Christmas'.

ith proper protection and care, it is possible to sustain an amaryllis bulb for ten years or more.

producing flowers altogether, especially if it is producing offset bulblets. As the mother bulb expires, the offsets are generally ready to produce their own flowers.

When the flowering season is over, you will notice that the bulb has shrunk from its original size, having expended all its energy to make the flowers. The outer layers, or scales, dry out and become papery, and you can peel them off above the soil line, revealing the first solid green or white layer of the bulb. Sometimes the whole dried layer will slip away from the bulb and out of the soil if given a slight tug. Even if left alone the dried outer layers will eventually flake off and disintegrate; however, removing them inhibits pests that might take up residence between the dry scales.

The plant's foliage is critical to its rejuvenation process. Your goal is to fill the plant with food to promote the production of as many leaves as possible. Most plants produce from four to a dozen leaves. A well-fed bulb will start to form additional scales, and new leaves will appear. Most horticulturists believe that it takes four leaves to produce one flower scape, as the flower buds arise in the axils of every fourth bulb scale.

Root production also affects performance. If your bulb arrived from the supplier with no roots or very few, it may skip flowering the second year, as it has to invest its food into making new roots.

Amaryllis are voracious eaters. Observe a regular feed-

Right: 'Charmeur'. Overleaf: left, 'Dancing Queen'; right, 'Basuto'.

PLANTING AMARYLLIS IN THE GARDEN

If you live in Zones 9 to 11, you may transfer your amaryllis into the ground after they have bloomed indoors and cultivate them as garden plants. Lift the bulbs from their containers, shake the soil from their roots, and plant them about a foot apart in a well-drained location. The tops should be barely covered with soil. A soil rich in organic matter will promote good growth.

During a growing season, fertilize first when new growth appears, then again when the flower stem is 6 to 8 inches tall, and a third application when the old flower heads and stems have been removed. Use either a bulb booster fertilizer or a liquid fertilizer low in nitrogen, such as one with 5-10-10 or 6-12-12 analysis. Excess nitrogen promotes vegetative growth and reduces flowering. When the beds become crowded, divide the plants in the fall after the foliage turns yellow and begins to droop.

Photograph courtesy Dr. Alan W. Meerow

PESTS AND DISEASES

Amaryllis are remarkably free from pests and diseases, particularly if you do not overwater your plant and you provide good ventilation and moderate humidity. I keep my greenhouse cool at night (50 to 60 degrees), which probably slows down my amaryllis performance speed, but I believe those temperatures discourage pests and disease. Nonetheless, there are a few problems to watch for:

FIRE OR RED LEAF SPOT, RED BLOTCH, OR LEAF SCORCH—*Stagonospora curtisii*

The most common potential disease for the amaryllis is one that appears as red spots, lesions, or cankers on leaves, flower stems, and flowers. Infected stalks and leaves may grow at an angle to the main axis. Leaves or stems may be deformed and the bulb may have red blotches, which rot easily. Young cankers are bright red; as they elongate the center becomes soft, sunken, and brown. Red Blotch is exacerbated by warm, humid conditions. Discard diseased bulbs and the soil in which they were planted.

BULB ROT—*Botrytis cinerea*, *Rhizopus stolonifer*, *Sclerotium rolfsii*

Planting bulbs that are bruised or keeping the soil too wet promotes bulb and root rot. Discard rotted bulbs and their soil.

BULB ROT—*fusarium*

A fungus that causes rotting of the basal plate and roots, it is generally indicated by a softening of the bulb. Fusarium may also be identified by the presence of a sour odor or white mold on the exterior of the bulb. Avoid ammonium fertilizers, as they seem to encourage fusarium. Discard bulbs and their soil.

MOSAIC VIRUS—*hippeastrum mosaic potyvirus*

A disease that cannot be detected when the bulbs are leafless, it will reveal itself as soon as the leaves appear with irregular light green or yellow-green coloration in random striations on the darker green leaves. Discard diseased bulbs and their soil.

FUNGUS GNATS—*lycoriella mali*

Fungus gnats thrive in damp soil that is high in organic matter, where they live on fungi. If they cannot find other food sources, they may feed on plant roots and cause stunting of the bulb and flower. Allowing the pot to dry out between waterings is the best preventative. If an invasion arrives, try using the organic *Bacillus thuringensis isaelensis* (Bti H-14), which controls the larvae, as a soil drench. It is commercially available under the names Gnatrol or Knock-Out Gnats.

MITES *Tetranychus bimachulatus, Tarsonemus laticeps, Rhizoglyphus echinopus* **THRIPS** *Hercinothrips femoralis, Heliothrips haemorrhoidalis, Frankliniella tritici, Taeniothrips simplex* **MEALYBUGS** *Pseudococcus citri* **SOFT SCALE** *Coccus hesperidum* **BULB MITE SCALE** *Steneotarsonemus laticeps*

Spray with a solution of organic horticultural soap. Alternatively, apply a homemade remedy: mix a solution of one part alcohol to two parts water. Be aware that sprays may damage the delicate surfaces of the flower petals.

The disease Red Blotch shows on the edges of a 'Red Lion' flower spathe.

ing schedule throughout the plants' foliage-producing season, which will last three to five months, generally the duration of the summer. I fertilize my amaryllis biweekly as part of a monitoring and watering routine, but if you have the time, feeding them every week with a half-strength fertilizer is not extravagant.

Use a complete, water-soluble houseplant fertilizer, such as a 20-20-20 formula, which contains nitrogen (for strong, vigorous growth, good leaf color, and photosynthesis), phosphorus (for root growth and development), and potassium (for photosynthesis, uptake of other nutrients, and general good health). Avoid a fertilizer with ammonium nitrogen, the form nitrogen takes in some commercial fertilizers. You may use a fertilizer that has a higher phosphorus count, like 8-12-4 or 15-30-15. A good houseplant fertilizer will also contain trace elements, sometimes called micronutrients, such as iron and magnesium. Dampen the soil before applying fertilizer to ensure that you do not burn the roots. A good rule of thumb for a 5- to 8-inch pot is about a pint of liquid fertilizer biweekly.

When late-spring nighttime temperatures reach about 60 degrees, I line my amaryllis pots in a fenced courtyard outside the greenhouse, where they enjoy fresh air and filtered light for their summer vacation. Orient your amaryllis to receive morning sun, as it is more gentle; western afternoon sun can be brutally hot and scorching. Remember that small pots dry out quickly on a hot, windy day. Pots can also be inserted into the garden soil for the summer season, and will require less attention, but avoid placing them where they will become excessively dry. You may also remove the bulbs from their pots and plant them directly in the ground. They will love it, often producing more roots

than those in pots, but this method makes it harder to keep track of different varieties, as their labels can become mixed up or lost.

At summer's end, trim or remove any foliage that has turned yellow, flopped over, or dried out. To encourage the bulb to go dormant, stop fertilizing and gradually cease watering.

Storing Dormant Bulbs

Store your potted bulbs in a dry, cool (50 to 55 degrees) closet, garage, or basement. You can turn the pots on their sides and stack them like a pyramid or remove the bulbs from their pots altogether and store the bare bulbs in sand, vermiculite, or laid out on a bed of newspaper (keep them with their labels). Dig up any amaryllis you have planted in the garden for the summer and bring them indoors. If you are storing the roots open to the air, sprinkle them with water once a month to keep them alive. I generally store amaryllis, pot and all, on shelves. Since amaryllis resent root disturbance, it seems kinder—as well as easier—to leave them in their pots.

When all of the foliage has yellowed and dried, cut it

When the amaryllis dies down, it is
the plant's signal that it is filled with food
and, like a human at the
close of a gastronomical orgy, it needs a good nap—
in a frost-free location.

off to within an inch of the bulb top. If some foliage remains green, cut it off, too. At this point the plant requires two to three months of dormancy instead of producing additional foliage. Making foliage draws moisture from the bulb. For those amaryllis that slumber for three months rather than two, you should moisten the soil once a month, so that the roots do not shrivel.

If you have the resources to refrigerate the bulbs, you can duplicate the grower's methods. Remove the bulbs from their pots and store them in bins with air holes, and with the appropriate labels. Place in a refrigerator at 45 to 50 degrees for a minimum of six weeks. (Never store fruit, particularly apples, in the same refrigerator, as it gives off ethylene gas, which will sterilize your bulb and cause it to rot or to produce deformed flowers.)

Reviving Stored Bulbs

When October arrives, begin to bring the bulbs out in a staggered sequence. Most amaryllis will bloom six to twelve weeks from the time you begin to coax them out of their dormancy. Bring any amaryllis that already show growth out first, as they are raring to go. Pot the bulbs that you have stored bareroot, attending first to those that show the tips of their flower scapes.

Check that the bulbs you stored in their pots have room to grow. Even though amaryllis like to be snug in their pots, they increase in diameter as they age, and may need to be repotted every three or four years. To repot, remove the bulb from the soil and shake it off or wash it off with a gentle stream of water. Remove dry scales. Some growers recommend pruning the roots to five inches when repotting. Repot in the next size pot.

Since my amaryllis sleep in their pots, I like to freshen their appearance when I wake them up. Without disturbing the roots, I scratch out the loosest soil at the top of the pot and replace it with newly mixed planting medium. A tablespoon of bone meal mixed with the medium adds phosphorus to the soil. I may even rewrite the labels, if the previous year's exposure to water and light have made them look dingy.

All that remains is to water the bulb. If it was stored in a porous pot, like terra-cotta, I immerse it, pot and all, in water to about an inch from the top, until the pot stops hissing. Otherwise, if the bulb is in a glazed or plastic pot, give it a good watering. Place the amaryllis in a well-lighted room, and it will soon reward you with another season of enchantment.

The mature 'Reve' flower displays a vast range of subtle shading.

3

inside amaryllis

THE ANATOMY AND PROPAGATION OF HIPPEASTRUM

The amaryllis is technically classified as a tender, perennial herb. Taking the form of a bulb, it is included—along with tubers, rhizomes, and corms—in a group of plants botanists refer to as geophytes. The bulb is a marvel of self-sufficiency, sending forth leaves, a stalk, and flowers that in turn contain all the elements necessary for reproduction. Most hybrid amaryllis are self-fertile; in other words, when an amaryllis transfers its own pollen to the stigma, it is capable of setting seed. The pollen is heavy; in nature it is not carried across distances to another flower by the wind, but rather conveyed from one flower to the next by insects. In breeding—the creation of a hybrid or a cross—the process can be achieved by man, and since the stamens and pistils are large and obvious, hand pollination is relatively easy. Amaryllis can also be propagated by offset division or by cuttage—which makes a brief lesson in plant anatomy a useful side trip for those interested in prolonging the lives of their prize amaryllis or even experimenting in creating varieties of their own.

Flowering plants are divided into two classes: monocotyledons and dicotyledons. The amaryllis is classified among the monocotyledons, which typically have seeds with a single cotyledon, or seedleaf. Its foliage is narrow with parallel veins. The flower components come in multiples of three. The sepals, collectively called the calyx, are outermost; the petals, together called the corolla, form the inner circle and are sometimes narrower in form. Amaryllis' sepals and petals, which are together referred to as tepals, come in an enormous range of colors from the most pastel pink to vivid orange, from clear white to velvety red. Many, particularly when kissed by the sun, have an iridescent glow. The ridge in the center of each petal is the keel, shaped like that of a boat. Flowers are horizontal to drooping, trumpet-shaped, or borne in lily-like umbels. Some flowers are open-faced, while others are more closed and irregular, like orchids.

The life of the amaryllis plant consists of two phases. The immature, or purely

A cross section of a 'Ludwig Dazzler' bulb shows the fully formed flower bud that resides inside. Overleaf: left, 'Candy Floss'; right, 'Basuto'.

*u*nlike tulips or hyacinths, whose

roots die every year to be replaced the next, the roots of an amaryllis are always alive.

vegetative, phase begins with the germination of the seed, when a tiny bulb is formed, and progresses through a virtually continuous period of leaf production. When the upper portions of the leaves wither, they act as food storage organs. The mature phase consists of regular cycles of leaf growth and formation of the flower buds, which develop within the bulb and ultimately emerge to make the flowers. Most hybrids are deciduous, which means they go through two distinct annual stages: the first when flower and leaves are produced, and the second when the leaves come to maturity and die down, and the plant takes a rest.

Amaryllis bulbs vary in size, depending on age and type. A cone-shaped stem is located in the lower center of the bulb. It is surrounded by bulb scales: the inner, living ones are thick and fleshy; the outer ones dead, dry, and papery. Food reserves, carbohydrates, fats, and proteins, which are stored in the stem and living bulb scales, produce the leafless stalks, or scapes, which terminate with the inflorescences, or flower clusters.

The leaves are the source of essential carbohydrates, made from water absorbed from the roots and carbon dioxide from the air. Chlorophyll, the green coloring matter of plant cells, is the catalyst, and the sun is the power that generates the action.

Amaryllis produces fibrous roots, which are formed in a ring—the basal plate—around the lowest bulb scales. The roots function both by absorbing moisture and nutrients from the soil and by firmly gripping the soil to prevent the bulb from falling over as the flower stalk grows.

Left: 'Calimero'. Above: The ripe seed head of 'Red Lion'.

Amaryllis flowers are borne on leafless, hollow, round scapes, which are often covered with a fine powdery bloom. You will notice marks when you touch the stalk and disturb the powdery surface. The leaf-like parts immediately beneath the flower cluster are spathe valves; they wrap around the flower buds to protect them as they push forth from the bulb and split open as the buds inside increase in size. Greenish-white, yellowish, or pink while closed, the pods turn light brown and papery after the buds have emerged.

The plant's flower is the site of its sexual reproduction. The parts are arranged in whorls around the receptacle, located at the tip of the pedicel, known collectively as the perigone. The tepals—which we commonly refer to as petals—surround the male and female reproductive system: the androecium and gynoecium. The androecium consists collectively of six stamens, the male organs. Each stamen is made up of a filament stalk and a two-lobed anther; each lobe con-

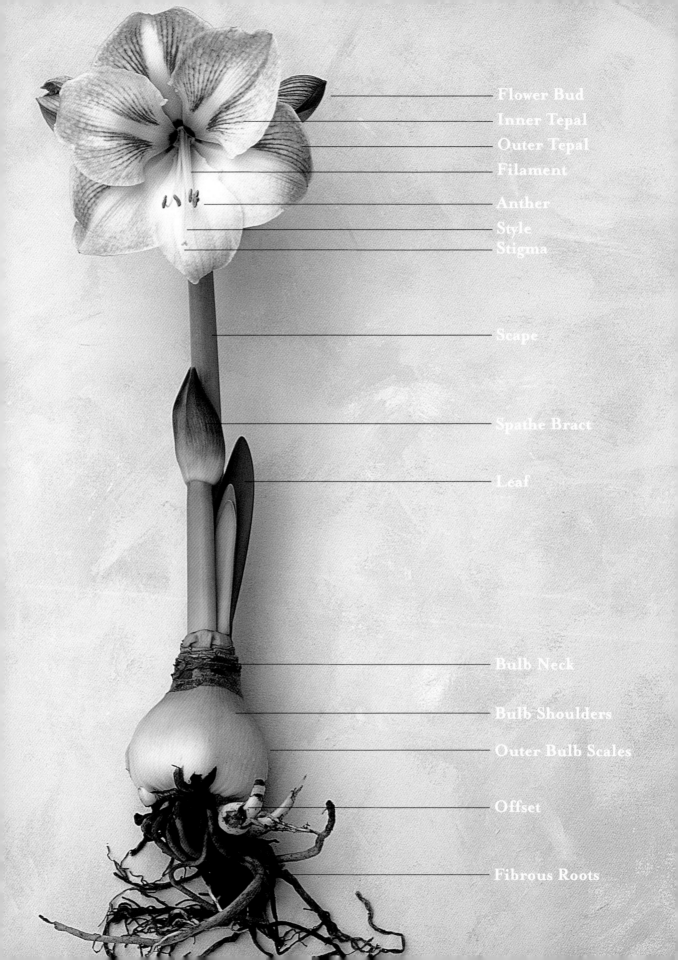

Flower Bud

Inner Tepal

Outer Tepal

Filament

Anther

Style
Stigma

Scape

Spathe Bract

Leaf

Bulb Neck

Bulb Shoulders

Outer Bulb Scales

Offset

Fibrous Roots

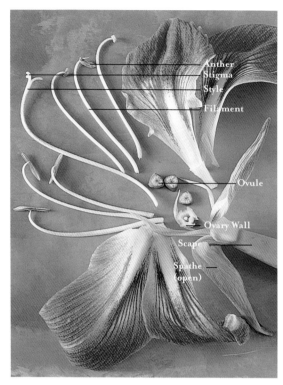

Anther
Stigma
Style
Filament
Ovule
Ovary Wall
Scape
Spathe (open)

Left: 'Candy Floss'. Opposite: 'Apple Blossom'. Overleaf: left, 'Aphrodite'; right, within the spathe valves the flowers—here 'Blushing Bride'—are grouped into an umbel with two to six flowers. Each flower is carried on a pedicel, a small stalk that supports that individual flower.

tains two pollen sacs. As the flower opens the anthers ripen, within hours exposing golden pollen grains. These house a generative cell, which produces two male gametes, each of which contains a male gamete nucleus, the mechanism that controls its operation, maintenance, and reproduction—including inherited genes.

The gynoecium, or female organ, is called a pistil and it consists of three parts. The first is the swollen basal portion, the ovary, located below the perigone and containing three hollow chambers, or locules. Within the perigone is a narrow, elongated style, on top of which is a three-forked, or triangularly lobed, stigma. When the flower has been open for a day, the stigma elongates and arches upward, separating gradually over the next three days into three prongs. The locules of the ovary generally contain many ovules from which the egg, or female gamete, develops. It, in turn, contains the egg nucleus.

In pollination the male pollen grains are transferred to the surface of the female stigma. When the pollen reaches the stigma, a tube begins to form. The pollen tube elongates on the exterior of the stigma, enters it, and grows through the tissues of the style to reach the ovary—and the ovules that contain the eggs. When fertilization occurs, a microscopic zygote is created, which may—by repeated cell division—develop into the embryo and, ultimately, a plantlet. The embryo is part of the seed, which in the case of the amaryllis is dry, black or dark brown, flat and papery, and shaped like the letter D.

The dry three-chambered structure containing the seeds, into which the ovary matures, is called the capsule. When it is fully ripe, the chamber bursts open and frees the seeds—papery brown seed scales that, when fertile, house seeds—which will be carried to their future homes for germination by the wind, or by hand.

Propagation Three Ways: Seed, Offset, and Cuttage

Having successfully grown amaryllis and nurtured them back to repeat their performances in subsequent winters, the logical next step is the desire to propagate. It is tempting to look at the flowers you favor and want to nudge their plants to procreate. Three ways, with some variations, will bring you amaryllis babies.

BY SEED

If you have left the anthers on your flower and allowed the pollen to ripen and pollinate the ovary, your plant will produce a seed head in about four to five weeks. (Allowing your amaryllis to set seed saps energy from the bulb.) The amaryllis will quickly let you know if it has been pollinated. The smooth green area at the end of the flower will swell within a week and begin to take on a spherical form, gradually changing to a three-segmented structure.

After the seed head ripens, turns yellow, and splits

open, the seeds can be harvested. Seeds should be removed from the pod, then allowed to air-dry at room temperature for a few days. Amaryllis seeds, even stored in ideal conditions—in unsealed envelopes or open containers—retain their viability for only a short time, especially in humid climates, so plant as soon as possible. Before planting, presoak the seeds by floating them on water for twelve hours or overnight.

Plant the seeds indoors at any season in a well-drained, sterilized medium in a seed tray. Sow them on their sides or with the long straight edge downward and the rounded edge protruding slightly from the soil. Some growers place glass or plastic over the top of the container to create incubating conditions in which the humidity in the air and the moisture in the growing medium remain constant. Punching a few air holes allows ventilation and prevents seeds from molding and

seedlings from "damping off," a term for soil diseases that cause seeds to rot or seedlings to collapse. Bottom heat in the form of an electric heating pad will encourage speedy germination. Germination will take two to six weeks.

After the seedling sprouts a small, blade-like leaf, feed the plant biweekly with a complete fertilizer like 5-10-5; water after each application. When seedlings have produced two or three leaves, transplant into 3-inch pots. Your seedlings should flower in two to four years. Seeds from hybrids will rarely come true, making seed sowing an unpredictable method of propagation.

OFFSET DIVISION

If your amaryllis bulb has been grown for two or more years, it may produce a bulblet, referred to as an offset or "daughter." The offset derived through this vegetative reproduction is called a clone. Hybrids, which have gone under intensive breeding programs, are often slower to produce offsets than the species; some, like 'Red Lion' and 'Clown', rarely spawn children. Since a plant with offsets may be crowded in its pot, you may transfer the bulb and its babies to a larger pot, giving it room to expand with its offspring attached. A bulb family joined at its hips may even flower stunningly in unison, though ultimately the mother bulb may shrivel and give way to the offsets.

You may wait, as some growers do, for the offsets to separate from the mother bulb naturally, but they may also be divided if the offset has grown to the size of a small onion and developed a separate root system. Divide right after the bulbs' dormant period. Carefully shake the soil off the roots, and separate the bulblets

Left and opposite, right: Tiny bulblets are beginning to form and then develop around the basal plate of a mother bulb. Opposite, above: When slicing the bulb in sections for the cuttage method of propagation, be sure roots are left on each portion.

from the mother bulb, either by cutting apart with a clean, sharp, sterilized knife or by gently pulling the offset away from the mother, being careful not to damage the roots.

Allow the offset bulbs to rest for a couple of weeks in a dry, vented container, such as a cardboard box with holes in it. Replant the bulbs in individual pots just as you would mature amaryllis. Be sure that the offset's neck is above the soil line. The babies will take two to four years to reach the stage where they produce the four leaves needed to generate flowers, and most remain in a continuous vegetative state until then. But if their foliage dies back, they are asking for a rest; allow them to go dormant, just as you would mature bulbs.

CUTTAGE OR TWIN-SCALING

If you prefer not to wait for your bulb to produce offsets or it is a variety that does not make them, you can make new plants by cutting an existing bulb into multiple sections.

The optimum time for propagation by cuttage, also called twin-scaling, is from August to November, when the bulb tissues contain the greatest reserves of food. Choose a mature, healthy bulb that has demonstrated vigorous growth. Cut the bulb vertically into narrow wedges containing two scales, the number of wedges depending on the size of your bulb. Each piece must retain a portion of the stem tissue or basal plate attached to the scales to remain viable.

Allow the wedge to dry for forty-eight hours so that the wound can heal. Plant the wedge in a mixture of

two parts peat and one part sand or in moistened vermiculite. Water the pot by standing it in a tray containing an inch or so of water, so it can wick up the desired amount from the bottom. This avoids getting water on the cut bulb, which can cause bulb rot. As in the case of seedlings, heat from the bottom will accelerate growth. Keep the cuttings shaded from direct sun and in an area with a high level of humidity. With luck, offsets will begin to grow in two to six months.

Another cuttage method that stimulates the bulb to produce offshoots is to remove the center of the basal plate, just as you might core one end of an apple. First, using a knife, cut off the roots, without damaging the basal plate. Scoop out the core—about $1\frac{1}{2}$ inches into the bulb—or you may fashion a tool by sharpening the edges of a spoon with a fine file. Then slice the

bulb about a third of the way up the sides, leaving the neck intact. Force a separation between the wedges by inserting sections of thin wooden tongue depressors; otherwise the sliced sides may heal back together. Fill the hole in the center with sand. The excised center core can also be planted.

Prepare a pot for correct drainage and fill halfway up with equal parts well-drained sterilized medium and sand. Set the bulb on the medium and add straight sand to cover the tops of the cuts. Since this bulb no longer has roots for water intake, you must keep the soil evenly moist, but not soggy. Too much water will cause bulb rot. Root growth will occur simultaneously with the formation of new bulblets. When the bulblets reach the point that they are making their own roots—you can tell by giving the bulblet a very gentle tug, and it will feel secure—you should begin fertilizing.

A third method is to make wedge-shaped cuts across the basal plate. Use your knife to cut inch-deep wedges extending from the center of the basal plate to the side of the bulb. Let the cuts dry for forty-eight hours and plant in sterilized potting soil, again mixed with sand. Bulblets should appear in the wedges in about six months. Bottom heat helps with both of these methods as well.

Hybridizing

If you enjoy a challenge, you may try your hand at creating your own cross or hybrid. Choose two amaryllis whose characteristics you admire—keeping in mind that in this lottery you may well end up with a plant bearing the least attractive characteristics of each. However, the good news is that you could end up with a unique beauty or new plant that has a flower larger than either of the parents had, a phenomenon called hybrid vigor.

To create a hybrid, you need to transfer the pollen of one flower to the stigma of another so the female and male gametes in the ovule can produce a zygote.

1. Choose one parent to give the pollen. Remove the anthers from the flower as soon as it opens and place them in a small glass or porcelain jar. The anthers will ripen and shrink, releasing the fine, bright yellow pollen, which will collect in the bottom of the jar. Allow the pollen to dry for twelve to twenty-four hours with the container top slightly ajar; mold can develop in a sealed jar. A small amount—a pinch—of calcium chloride in the bottom of the jar will hasten the drying process. Label the jar with the plant name and the date collected. If it is kept at room temperature, the pollen remains viable for up to a week. Refrigerated, pollen remains viable for a few months, and frozen, a year or more.

2. Choose another parent for the seed. Remove the anthers from the flower as soon as it opens, and either discard them or collect them as in step 1 for use in another cross. The stigma must be mature—elongated and pointing upward—before it will successfully receive pollination. Generally, it exudes a sticky substance that makes the pollen adhere to it. However, if a bead of stigmatic fluid is visible, the flower is past peak receptivity. If the process is to be done outdoors, professional breeders recommend placing a paper bag over the flower head and tying it with a string at the base while the stigma is maturing to prevent insects from pollinating it from an unwanted flower. In a greenhouse, the bag is unnecessary.

3. Using either a small paintbrush or your finger, pick up the pollen from the jar and gently rub it on the entire surface of the female flower's stigma. Label your cross. If you are using a paper bag, immediately replace it over the flower; when the flower has faded, the bag may be removed. Wait for the seed head to be produced, and then follow the instructions above for drying and sowing the seed. (For self-pollination of the hybrid amaryllis, place the pollen from the same flower on its own stigma in the method described above. A flower that is prolific with pollen may even pollinate itself.)

The anthers and stigma are fully mature on a 'Lemon Lime' flower.

what's in a name?

A GLOSSARY OF HIPPEASTRUM HYBRIDS

Amaryllis hybrids come in a vast array of sizes, shapes, and colors, and in single and double forms. Some flowers have flat open faces with broad, rounded petals that may reflex at the tips. Others have narrower, pointed petals that project forward. The blooms range in size from 4 inches, as in the vermilion miniature 'Calimero', to 8 or 10 inches, like the boldly striped 'Clown'. Stems top out anywhere from 8 to 30 inches. Normally each flower scape will produce four flowers; however, some have as few as two, and a few, like 'Floris Hecker' and 'Charmeur', produce as many as six.

Since so many bulbs are imports from countries using the metric system, they are measured and graded in centimeters, 26 to 28 centimeters, measured at their widest circumference, being a common size. In inches, that translates to about $9^1/2$ to $10^1/2$ inches around. Miniatures may be smaller. Larger, older bulbs may measure 34 to 36 centimeters ($13^1/2$ to $14^1/4$ inches) or more; labeled "giant," "jumbo," or "superbulbs," they produce multiple flower scapes, and thus more flowers and an extended season of performance. A six- or seven-year-old "mother" bulb's waistline may be a whopping 40 centimeters (16 inches).

Amaryllis habits vary, too, depending on the dominant characteristics of their parentage. Many hybrids unfurl in an upturned position and then mature to widely opened face, but others, like the bright pink 'Bestseller', remain cupped until their flowers fade. The elegant white 'Intokazi's' head remains always slightly bent. Like the burst of a firecracker, 'Andes', a salmon-and-white double, opens and holds its flowers permanently in an upturned position. Aloft tall scapes, the small clusters of 'Amoretta's' flowers seem to soar like birds freed in an indoor garden.

Double flowering refers to the number of petals—twice as many as in a single hybrid—in each flower, and over the last ten years breeders have concentrated on creating new cultivars of these bouquets on stems. Many of the doubles, like the mighty 'Aphrodite' or the proud 'White Peacock', open with sharply pointed petals that mature over a few days to softly rippled edges. 'Snow White' has draped ruffles, making the number of petals appear infinite, rather than a mere dozen.

The floriferous 'Floris Hecker' consistently produced a half dozen flawless flowers on every stem. Overleaf: left, 'Charmeur'; right, 'Prins Carnival'.

*W*hile amaryllis range in color from

the pastel pink of 'First Love' to the bold tangerine-striped 'Toronto', the differences between similarly colored hybrids can be very subtle.

'Orange Sovereign' flames in red-orange, but 'Eos' is a true, clear orange. 'Rilona' and 'Charmeur' are both salmon, but 'Rilona' leans lightly toward peach, while 'Charmeur' suggests persimmon. 'Charmeur' and 'Nagano' are exactly the same color, but 'Nagano' is more delicate in form and bearing.

Some amaryllis—'Fairy Tale' and 'Blazing Star', to name two—wear sharply defined stripes, but others have more irregular markings: 'Cinderella' boasts kitten whiskers drawn on an upturned face, 'Charisma' is speckled with cranberry dots that fade to a creamy background, while 'Elvas' and 'Allure' seem splashed with the juice of sweet cherries. A white star often distinguishes the blossoms' faces, as on the carmine petals of 'Cocktail'. That bold star shape was clearly the inspiration for naming both 'Baby Star' and 'Bright Star'. 'Picotee'—its name aptly derived from the French word *picoté,* meaning marked with tiny points—has pristine white petals edged with a fine crimson line. Petal textures range from the seersucker crinkles of 'Susan's' face to the porcelain-like surface of 'Nymph'.

The inclusion of the words *purple, lavender,* or *lilac* in the names of some hybrids reflects growers' desire to extend the available palette of amaryllis, but such labels are largely wishful thinking. 'Lilac Wonder' remains one of the most gorgeous varieties, but no amount of hyperbole can change its coat from pink-veined apricot with a hint of lavender to a true lilac. 'Royal Purple' is a regal lady in every way, but her cloak is deep bluish-pink, not purple.

The industry has been more successful in pursuing

the coveted color yellow, 'Germa' and 'Yellow Pioneer' being standouts. Both are yellow, floriferous, long-flowering, and elegant. True to its name, dainty 'Lemon Lime' is greenish-yellow.

Amaryllis names can hark to their birthrights, as well as to their personalities. 'Basuto', 'Intokazi', and 'Heart of Kenya' are African, while 'Star of Holland' hails, of course, from the Netherlands. Those touted as "Christmas flowering" probably originate in South Africa; since plants imported from the southern hemisphere will observe the calendar of their origins during the first year in their new homes. Your African amaryllis will blossom in its spring—fall and winter in North America. Planted in October, or even November, they

Left: 'Elvas' in full flower. Right: 'Ludwig Dazzler'.
Overleaf: left, 'Noel'; right, 'Heart of Kenya'.

The Dutch hybrids follow the schedule of their adopted habitat and flower in early spring. Most come into bloom eight to twelve weeks after planting.

are groomed for immediate performance and will flash and glow throughout the holiday season. Allow them four to six weeks from planting to flowering. For me, 'Basuto', 'Candy Floss', and 'Cocktail' all bloomed four weeks after planting, and the speedy 'Intokazi' produced its first flower in a mere twenty-five days. Of course, there are exceptions to every rule: 'Masai' took its time. In the beginning of March, when the African season in my studio was just a memory, 'Masai', a tall, single white, finally made its imperial appearance.

Even from the best suppliers one can expect some inconsistency and inaccuracy in labeling. Some bulbs are simply mismarked; others, having been through extensive hybridization, can be aberrations of their varieties. The more variegated the cultivar is, the more irregularly colored the flowers may be from bulb to bulb. 'Blossom Peacock' can be dominantly white with splotches of cranberry or it can be the opposite. Out of three bulbs of 'Razzmatazz' I purchased from the same source, one was red- and white-striped, which matches the variety's description in the catalog, and two bloomed in solid red, with no touch of white at all. 'Naughty Lady', as if flaunting her feisty name, came dressed in different shades of peach, as well as pink.

Even more discrepancies occur between the same named hybrids purchased from different sources.

Opposite: 'Fairy Tale'. Overleaf: left, 'Charmeur'; right, 'Blossom Peacock'.

'Susan', while not failing to wear pink, grew to 12 inches and presented a small upturned face from one supplier; she shot to 24 inches with noble bearing and large open face from another.

Furthermore, some growers give different names to identical-looking hybrids in order to make their offerings seem unique. I could see no difference between the creamy 'White Christmas' bought from one supplier and its twin, 'Denver', purchased from another; the same was true of 'Rosy Frills', 'Double Record', and 'Lady Jane', all ruffled double pinks. 'Wonderland' and 'Las Vegas' are so close in coloration and markings to the popular standby 'Apple Blossom', a cultivar dating to 1954, that they could be its clones.

While the large pansy-faced or trumpet-shaped hybrids are the most prevalent, miniatures are increasingly sought for their size and natural grace. They are often more free-flowering, producing one flower scape after another. Some yellow-and-green-flowering cultivars, like 'Green Goddess' and 'Lemon Lime', and the brightly colored 'Pamela' and 'Baby Star', which were developed from *H. gracilis* or *H. striatum*, are classified as "gracilis" types because of their diminutive size. The Brazilian *H. papilio*, aptly also called the butterfly amaryllis, is finicky, sometimes refusing to bloom altogether, but its delicate downturned face, patterned with lime green and mahogany stripes, remains irresistible—perhaps my personal favorite.

*W*hatever your
preferences—open dinner plate or
drooping lily-like flower form, colors
from the most fragile pink
to bold vermilion red, tall or
short stature, single or double,
early or late blooming—the stately
amaryllis offers
a choice for every occasion
throughout the
winter season.

glossary of hippeastrum hybrids

Amoretta
Miniature
Height: 18 inches
Flower size: $4^{1}/_{2}$ inches
From planting to
flowering: 4 weeks

Opposite: 'Rilona'.

Allure
Dutch hybrid—double flowering
Height: 16 inches
Flower size: 7 inches
From planting to flowering: 7 weeks

Angelique
Dutch hybrid—single flowering
Height: 20 inches
Flower size: 7 inches
From planting to flowering: 8 weeks

Ambiance
Dutch hybrid—single flowering
Height: 14 inches
Flower size: 7 inches
From planting to flowering: 16 weeks

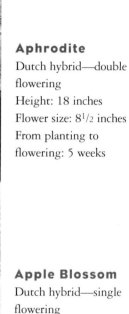

Aphrodite
Dutch hybrid—double flowering
Height: 18 inches
Flower size: $8^{1}/_{2}$ inches
From planting to flowering: 5 weeks

Amigo
Dutch hybrid—single flowering
Height: 16 inches
Flower size: 6 inches
From planting to flowering: 8 weeks

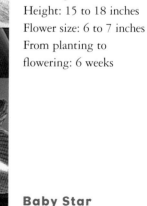

Apple Blossom
Dutch hybrid—single flowering
Height: 15 to 18 inches
Flower size: 6 to 7 inches
From planting to flowering: 6 weeks

Andes
Dutch hybrid—double flowering
Height: 12 to 14 inches
Flower size: $5^{1}/_{2}$ to 6 inches
From planting to flowering: 4 weeks

Baby Star
Miniature
Height: 24 to 26 inches
Flower size: 5 inches
From planting to flowering: 4 weeks

Basuto

African hybrid—single
flowering
Height: 12 to 18 inches
Flower size: 7 to 8 inches
From planting to
flowering: 4 weeks

Blushing Bride

African hybrid—double
flowering
Height: 12 to 16 inches
Flower size: 6^1/$_2$ inches to
7^1/$_2$ inches
From planting to
flowering: 4 weeks

Bestseller

Dutch hybrid—single
flowering
Height: 12 to 14 inches
Flower size: 5 to 6 inches
From planting to
flowering: 12 weeks

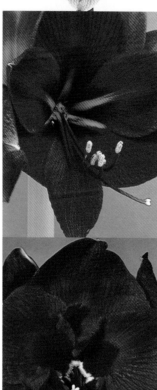

Bolero

Dutch hybrid—single
flowering
Height: 14 inches
Flower size: 6 inches
From planting to
flowering: 10 weeks

Blazing Star

African hybrid—single
flowering
Height: 20 to 26 inches
Flower size: 6 to 7^1/$_2$
inches
From planting to
flowering: 6 weeks

Bold Leader

African hybrid—single
flowering
Height: 12 to 16 inches
Flower size: 7 inches
From planting to
flowering: 4 weeks

Blossom Peacock

Dutch hybrid—double
flowering
Height: 14 to 18 inches
Flower size: 5 to 6 inches
From planting to
flowering: 7 weeks

Bright Star

Miniature
Height: 18 to 20 inches
Flower size: 5 inches
From planting to
flowering: 5 weeks

Calimero

Miniature
Height: 16 to 18 inches
Flower size: 4 to $4^{1}/_{2}$ inches
From planting to flowering: 4 weeks

Candy Floss

African hybrid—single flowering
Height: 16 to 20 inches
Flower size: 7 inches
From planting to flowering: 4 weeks

Carina

Miniature
Height: 18 inches
Flower size: $4^{1}/_{2}$ inches
From planting to flowering: 5 weeks

Charisma

Dutch hybrid—single flowering
Height: 14 to 16 inches
Flower size: 6 inches
From planting to flowering: 12 weeks

Charmeur

Dutch hybrid—single flowering
Height: 18 inches
Flower size: $6^{1}/_{2}$ to 7 inches
From planting to flowering: 6 weeks

Christmas Gift

Dutch hybrid—single flowering
Height: 10 to 14 inches
Flower size: 6 to $7^{1}/_{2}$ inches
From planting to flowering: 12 weeks

Cinderella

Dutch hybrid—single flowering
Height: 12 to 14 inches
Flower size: $5^{1}/_{2}$ to 6 inches
From planting to flowering: 16 weeks

Clown

Dutch hybrid—single flowering
Height: 22 to 24 inches
Flower size: 8 to 10 inches
From planting to flowering: 5 weeks

Cocktail
African hybrid—single
flowering
Height: 20 inches
Flower size: $7^1/_2$ to
$8^1/_2$ inches
From planting to
flowering: 4 weeks

Elvas
Dutch hybrid—double
flowering
Height: 12 to 20 inches
Flower size: 6 to
$7^1/_2$ inches
From planting to
flowering: 7 weeks

Dancing Queen
Dutch hybrid—double
flowering
Height: 24 inches
Flower size: 6 inches
From planting to
flowering: unknown,
purchased as a cut flower

Emerald
Miniature
Height: 14 to 16 inches
Flower size: 5 inches
From planting to
flowering: 8 weeks

Denver
Dutch hybrid—single
flowering
Height: 20 inches
Flower size: 7 inches
From planting to
flowering: 10 weeks

Eos
Dutch hybrid—single
flowering
Height: 16 inches
Flower size: 7 inches
From planting to
flowering: 12 weeks

Double Record
Dutch hybrid—double
flowering
Height: 12 to 14 inches
Flower size: 7 inches
From planting to
flowering: 8 weeks

Fairy Tale
Miniature
Height: 18 inches
Flower size: $4^1/_2$ inches
From planting to
flowering: 8 weeks

First Love

African hybrid—double flowering
Height: 12 to 16 inches
Flower size: 7¹/₂ to 8 inches
From planting to flowering: 6 weeks

Green Goddess

Miniature
Height: 15 to 16 inches
Flower size: 5¹/₂ to 7¹/₂ inches
From planting to flowering: 16 weeks

Floris Hecker

Dutch hybrid—single flowering
Height: 12 to 18 inches
Flower size: 5¹/₂ to 6¹/₂ inches
From planting to flowering: 7 weeks

Heart of Kenya

African hybrid—double flowering
Height: 16 to 20 inches
Flower size: 7 to 9 inches
From planting to flowering: 25 days

Germa

Miniature
Height: 10 to 14 inches
Flower size: 5¹/₂ inches
From planting to flowering: 5 weeks

Hercules

Dutch hybrid—single flowering
Height: 15 inches
Flower size: 7 inches
From planting to flowering: 12 weeks

Giraffe

Miniature
Height: 12 to 14 inches
Flower size: 4 to 4¹/₂ inches
From planting to flowering: 6 weeks

Hermitage

Dutch hybrid—single flowering
Height: 18 to 24 inches
Flower size: 7¹/₂ to 8¹/₂ inches
From planting to flowering: 12 weeks

Intokazi
African hybrid—single
flowering
Height: 24 inches
Flower size: 8 inches
From planting to
flowering: 25 days

Las Vegas
Dutch hybrid—single
flowering
Height: 16 inches
Flower size: 6 inches
From planting to
flowering: 6 weeks

Jaguar
Dutch hybrid—single
flowering
Height: 22 inches
Flower size: 5^1/$_2$ inches
From planting to
flowering: 12 weeks

Lemon Lime
Miniature
Height: 12 to 20 inches
Flower size: 5^1/$_2$ inches
From planting to
flowering: 8 weeks

Jewel
Dutch hybrid—double
flowering
Height: 10 to 20 inches
Flower size: 5 inches
From planting to
flowering: 8 weeks

Liberty
Dutch hybrid—single
flowering
Height: 12 inches
Flower size: 5^1/$_2$ to
6 inches
From planting to
flowering: 12 weeks

Lady Jane
Dutch hybrid—double
flowering
Height: 12 to 14 inches
Flower size: 7 inches
From planting to
flowering: 8 weeks

Lilac Wonder
Dutch hybrid—single
flowering
Height: 18 to 24 inches
Flower size: 7 to 8 inches
From planting to
flowering: 12 weeks

Ludwig Dazzler
Dutch hybrid—single flowering
Height: 12 to 14 inches
Flower size: 5 inches
From planting to flowering: 5 weeks

Masai
African hybrid—single flowering
Height: 22 inches
Flower size: $7^{1}/_{2}$ to 8 inches
From planting to flowering: 18 weeks

Merry Christmas
African hybrid—single flowering
Height: 10 to 14 inches
Flower size: $4^{1}/_{2}$ to 6 inches
From planting to flowering: 5 weeks

Milady
African hybrid—single flowering
Height: 10 to 14 inches
Flower size: $5^{1}/_{2}$ to 6 inches
From planting to flowering: 20 days

Miracle
African hybrid—single flowering
Height: 14 to 16 inches
Flower size: 5 to $6^{1}/_{2}$ inches
From planting to flowering: 6 weeks

Minerva
Dutch hybrid—single flowering
Height: 12 to 14 inches
Flower size: $5^{1}/_{2}$ inches
From planting to flowering: 14 weeks

Nagano
Dutch hybrid—single flowering
Height: 20 inches
Flower size: 6 inches
From planting to flowering: 9 weeks

Naughty Lady
Dutch hybrid—single flowering
Height: 14 to 26 inches
Flower size: 6 to $7^{1}/_{2}$ inches
From planting to flowering: 8 weeks

Noel

African hybrid—single
flowering
Height: 12 to 14 inches
Flower size: 6¹/₂ to
7 inches
From planting to
flowering: 4 weeks

Papilio

Miniature
Height: 12 to 14 inches
Flower size: 4 to 5 inches
From planting to
flowering: 8 weeks

Nymph

Dutch hybrid—double
flowering
Height: 6 to 12 inches
Flower size: 5 to 6 inches
From planting to
flowering: 7 weeks

Pasadena

Dutch hybrid – double
flowering
Height: 10 to 14 inches
Flower size: 5¹/₂ inches
From planting to
flowering: 7 weeks

Orange Sovereign

Dutch hybrid—single
flowering
Height: 22 to 24 inches
Flower size: 6¹/₂ to
7 inches
From planting to
flowering: 8 weeks

Philadelphia

Dutch hybrid—double
flowering
Height: 12 to 16 inches
Flower size: 7 inches
From planting to
flowering: 12 weeks

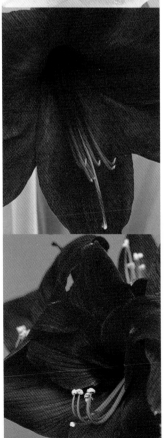

Pamela

Miniature
Height: 12 to 18 inches
Flower size: 5 inches
From planting to
flowering: 12 weeks

Picotee

Dutch hybrid—single
flowering
Height: 24 inches
Flower size: 6 inches
From planting to
flowering: 7 weeks

Pink Impressions

Dutch hybrid—single flowering

Height: 12 to 14 inches

Flower size: 5 to 6 inches

From planting to flowering: 16 weeks

Prins Carnival

Dutch hybrid—single flowering

Height: 12 to 14 inches

Flower size: 6 inches

From planting to flowering: 6 weeks

Ragtime

African hybrid—double flowering

Height: 10 to 12 inches

Flower size: 9 inches

From planting to flowering: 5 weeks

Rainbow

Dutch hybrid—double flowering

Height: 10 to 16 inches

Flower size: 6 to 7 inches

From planting to flowering: 5 weeks

Razzmatazz

African hybrid—double flowering

Height: 12 to 14 inches

Flower size: $5^1/_2$ to 6 inches

From planting to flowering: 4 weeks

RazzleDazzle

African hybrid—single flowering

Height: 14 inches

Flower size: $5^1/_2$ to 6 inches

From planting to flowering: 5 weeks

Red Charm

Dutch hybrid—single flowering

Height: 12 inches

Flower size: 5 inches

From planting to flowering: 12 weeks

Red Lion

Dutch hybrid—single flowering

Height: 24 inches

Flower size: 6 to 7 inches

From planting to flowering: 5 weeks

Red Peacock
Dutch hybrid—double flowering
Height: 14 to 16 inches
Flower size: 5 to 6 inches
From planting to flowering: 7 weeks

Red Sensation
Dutch hybrid—single flowering
Height: 12 to 14 inches
Flower size: $5^{1}/_{2}$ to 6 inches
From planting to flowering: 16 weeks

Reve
Dutch hybrid—single flowering
Height: 16 to 20 inches
Flower size: 6 inches
From planting to flowering: unknown, purchased as a cut flower

Rilona
Dutch hybrid—single flowering
Height: 18 inches
Flower size: 6 to 7 inches
From planting to flowering: 20 weeks

Rosy Frills
Dutch hybrid—double flowering
Height: 10 to 14 inches
Flower size: 7 inches
From planting to flowering: 9 weeks

Royal Purple
African hybrid—single flowering
Height: 14 inches
Flower size: 6 inches
From planting to flowering: 4 weeks

Royal Velvet
Dutch hybrid—single flowering
Height: 16 to 18 inches
Flower size: 6 inches
From planting to flowering: 10 weeks

Rozetta
African hybrid—double flowering
Height: 10 to 12 inches
Flower size: 8 inches
From planting to flowering: 4 weeks

Sandra
Dutch hybrid—single
flowering
Height: 12 to 14 inches
Flower size: 5 inches
From planting to
flowering: 8 weeks

Summertime
African hybrid—single
flowering
Height: 14 to 16 inches
Flower size: 6 to 8 inches
From planting to
flowering: 6 weeks

Scarlet Baby
Miniature
Height: 14 inches
Flower size: 4 inches
From planting to
flowering: 8 weeks

Sunrise
Dutch hybrid—single
flowering
Height: 20 inches
Flower size: 7¹/₂ to 8
inches
From planting to
flowering: unknown,
purchased as a cut flower

Snow White
African hybrid—double
flowering
Height: 12 to 16 inches
Flower size: 6 to 8 inches
From planting to
flowering: 4 weeks

Susan
Dutch hybrid—single
flowering
Height: 12 to 20 inches
Flower size: 6 to 8 inches
From planting to
flowering: 8 to 16 weeks

Star of Holland
Dutch hybrid—single
flowering
Height: 16 to 18 inches
Flower size: 6 to 7 inches
From planting to
flowering: 16 weeks

Sweet Surrender
Dutch hybrid—double
flowering
Height: 14 to 16 inches
Flower size: 7 to 9 inches
From planting to
flowering: 9 weeks

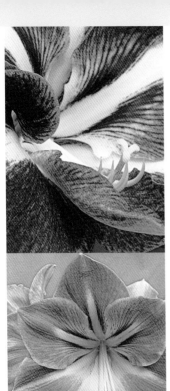

Toronto
Dutch hybrid—single
flowering
Height: 16 inches
Flower size: 6 to 7 inches
From planting to
flowering: 12 weeks

White Christmas
Dutch hybrid – single
flowering
Height: 20 inches
Flower size: 7 inches
From planting to
flowering: 12 weeks

Trendsetter
Dutch hybrid—single
flowering
Height: 14 inches
Flower size: 5 to 6 inches
From planting to
flowering: 6 weeks

White Peacock
Dutch hybrid—double
flowering
Height: 12 to 16 inches
Flower size: 8 inches
From planting to
flowering: 6 weeks

Vera
Dutch hybrid—single
flowering
Height: 14 to 18 inches
Flower size: 6 inches
From planting to
flowering: 6 weeks

Wonderland
Dutch hybrid—single
flowering
Height: 14 to 16 inches
Flower size: 6 inches
From planting to
flowering: 12 weeks

Wedding Dance
African hybrid—single
flowering
Height: 10 to 14 inches
Flower size: 5¹/₂ to
6 inches
From planting to
flowering: 7 weeks

Yellow Pioneer
Dutch hybrid—single
flowering
Height: 18 inches
Flower size: 6 to 7 inches
From planting to
flowering: 8 weeks

SOURCES

AMARYLLIS BULBS

Amaryllis Bulb Company
806 Avenue L, SC
Winter Haven, FL 33880
888-966-9866
Fax: 863-638-9699
www.amaryllis.com

McClure & Zimmerman
108 West Winnebago Street
P.O. Box 368
Friesland, WI 53935-0368
800-883-6998
Fax: 800-374-6120
www.mzbulb.com

Plant Delights Nursery, Inc.
9241 Sauls Road
Raleigh, NC 27603
919-772-4794
Fax: 919-662-0370
Hippeastrum × johnsonii
www.plantdelights.com

John Scheepers, Inc.
23 Tulip Drive
Bantam, CT 06750-1631
860-567-0838
Fax: 860-567-5323
www.johnscheepers.com

Smith & Hawken
P.O. Box 432
Milwaukee, WI 53201-0431
800-776-3336
www.SmithandHawken.com

K. van Bourgondien & Sons
245 Route 109
P.O. Box 1000
Babylon, NY 11702-9004
1-800-552-9996
Fax: 1-800-327-4268
www.kvbwholesale.com

Van Dyck's Flower
Bulbs and Perennials
P.O. Box 430
Brightwaters, NY 11718-0430
1-800-248-2852
Fax: 1-800-639-2452
www.vandycks.com

Van Engelen Inc.
23 Tulip Drive
Bantam, CT 06750
860-567-8734
Fax: 860-567-5323
www.vanengelen.com

White Flower Farm
P.O. Box 50
Litchfield, CT 06759-0050
30 Irene Street
800-503-9624
www.whiteflowerfarm.com

GREENHOUSE SUPPLIES

Charley's Greenhouse Supply
17979 State Route 536
Mount Vernon, WA 98273-3269
1-800-322-4707
Fax: 1-800-233-3078
www.charleysgreenhouse.com

Gardens Alive
5100 Schenley Place
Lawrenceburg, IN 47025
812-537-8650
Fax: 812-537-5108
www.gardensalive.com

Griffin Greenhouse
& Nursery Supplies
1619 Main Street
P.O. Box 36
Tewksbury, MA 01876
1-877-636-3623

Fax: 978-851-0012
www.griffins.com

MISCELLANEOUS

International Bulb Society
P.O. Box 92136
Pasadena, CA 91109-2136
www.bulbsociety.org

International Registration
Authority
Royal General Bulb Growers
Association Postbus 175
NL-2180 Ad Hillegom
The Netherlands

SELECTED BIBLIOGRAPHY

"Amaryllis." *Under Glass,* January–February, 1959.

Anderson, Dennis R. *American Flower Painting.* New York: Watson Guptill, 1980.

Anderson, William. "*Hippeastrums* for House Culture." *Horticulture,* March 15, 1931.

"Aristocrat." *The Floral Magazine,* December 1966.

Bailey, L. H. *Cyclopedia of American Horticulture,* vol. 2, E-M. New York: Macmillan, 1900.

Bainbridge, Richard. *Guide to the Conservatory: Being a Concise Treatise on the Management of the Hothouse and Greenhouse: the Forcing of Bulbs, Shrubs, etc.* London: R. Baldwin, 1842.

Blossfeld, Harry. "Breeding for Yellow Amaryllis Hybrids." *The Amaryllis Year Book, Plant Life 29,* 1973.

Blunt, Wilford, and William T. Stearn. *The Art of Botanical Illustration.* Woodbridge, Suffolk: The Antique Collector's Club, 1994.

Bowman, Jean. "Amaryllis: It's a Whale of a Bulb." *Plants Alive,* October 1978.

Brinhart, Betsy. "Amaryllis Trumpets Herald the Holidays." *The Floral Magazine,* November 1968.

Brown, Ken. "The Seductive Amaryllis." *Flower & Garden,* January/February 1997.

Bryan, John. *Bulbs,* Vol. 1, A–H. Portland, Ore.: Timber Press, 1989.

Bryan, John, consultant editor. *The New Royal Horticultural Society Manual of Bulbs.* London: Macmillan, 1995.

Caldwell, S. Y. "Growing the Large-Flowered Amaryllis." *Horticulture,* December 1, 1940.

Callaway, Dorothy J., and M. Brett. *Breeding Ornamental Plants.* Portland, Ore.: Timber Press, 2000.

Cothran, C. D. "Quest for Large Yellow Hippeastrum." *Herbertia* 41, 1985.

Cruso, Thalassa. "If I Love Amaryllis." *Horticulture,* November 1975.

Dickinson, Ina. "The No-Name Amaryllis." *Hobby Greenhouse,* Spring 1993.

Essen, James G. "*Hippeastrum* Hybridum." *Gardeners' Chronicle,* February 1938.

Hardman, Charles. "Trends in Modern *Hippeastrum* Hybridizing." International Bulb Society Publications. http://www.bulbsociety.org

Davis, Rosalie. "Potting and Growing Hybrid Amaryllis." *Horticulture,* November 1985.

De Hertogh, August. *Holland Bulb Forcer's Guide.* The Netherlands: Hillegom, 1985.

De Hertogh, August, and Marcel Le Nard. *The Physiology of Flower Bulbs: A Comprehensive Treatise on the Physiology and Utilization of Ornamental Flowering Bulbous and Tuberous Plants.* Amsterdam and New York: Elsevier, 1993.

DeWolf, Gordon. "Amaryllis." *Horticulture,* January 1983.

Doutt, Richard L. *Cape Bulbs.* Portland, Ore.: Timber Press, 1994.

Everett, Thomas H. *Illustrated Encyclopedia of Horticulture,* Vol. 1, A–Be; Vol. 5, G–Id. New York: New York Botanical Garden, Garland, 1981.

Faust, Joan Lee. "The Amaryllis Turns Brown Thumb Green." The *New York Times,* October 13, 1977.

———. "Amaryllis: Follow the Rules." The *New York Times,* September 17, 1989.

Fisher, John. *The Origins of Garden Plants.* London: Constable and Company, 1989.

Glattstein, Judy. "Winter-Flowering Amaryllis." *National Gardening,* November/December 1999.

Goedert, Robert D. "Amaryllid Culture." *The Amaryllis Year Book, Plant Life* 21, 1965.

———. "Hadeco Amaryllis Hybrids Grown in South Africa." *The Amaryllis Year Book, Plant Life* 17, 1961.

Hays, Robert M., and Janet Marinelli, editors. *Bulbs for Indoors: Year-Round Windowsill Splendor.* Brooklyn, N.Y.: The Brooklyn Botanic Garden, 1996.

Heaton, I. W. "History and Culture of Hybrid Amaryllis." *Flower Grower,* January 1936.

Herbert, William. *Amaryllidaceae: Preceded by an Attempt to Arrange the Monocotyledonous Orders, and Followed by a Treatise on Crossbred Vegetables, and Supplement.* London: J. Ridgway and Sons, 1837.

———. *An Appendix to the Botanical Register V. V1.* London: Ridgeway, 1821.

Hill, John. *Outlines of a System of Vegetable Generation.* London: Printed for the author, and to be had of R. Baldwin, 1758.

"Hippeastrums." *Your Garden,* December 1964.

Howie, Virginia. "Hybrid Amaryllis." *Horticulture,* February 1973.

Huxley, Anthony, editor. *The New Royal Horticultural Society Dictionary of Gardening,* vol. 2, D–K. London: The Macmillan Press, 1992.

Lack, H. Walter. *Garden Eden: Masterpieces of Botanical Illustration.* Köln: Taschen, 2001.

———. *A Garden for Eternity: The Codex Liechtenstein.* Berne: Benteli Publishers, 2001.

Linnaeus, Carl. *Hortus Cliffortianus.* New York: J. Cramer Lehre, 1968 reprint, originally published 1737.

———. *Species Planatarum.* Holmiae: Impensis L. Salvii, 1753.

Lorenz, Richard. *Imogen Cunningham: Flora.* Boston: A Bulfinch Press Book, 1996.

Mantegazza, Paolo. *The Legends of the Flowers.* New York: Wm. Farquhar Payson, n.d.

Martin, Laura C. *Garden Flower Folklore.* Chester, Conn.: The Globe Pequot Press, 1987.

Matthew, Brian, and Philip Swindells. *The Complete Book of Bulbs, Corms, Tubers, and Rhizomes.* Pleasantville, N.Y.: The Reader's Digest Association, 1994.

McCormick, Kathleen, and Michael Leccese. "Behold the Trumpet Amaryllis." The *New York Times,* December 24, 1995.

Meerow, Alan W. "Breeding Amaryllis." *Herbertia* 54, 1999.

———. "New Trends in Amaryllis (*Hippeastrum*) Breeding." *Proceedings of the Florida State Horticultural Society* 101, 1988.

———. "'Rio', 'Sampa', and 'Bahia', Three New Triploid Amaryllis Cultivars." *Horticultural Science* 35 (1), 2000.

Miller, John, and Kirsten Miller, editors. *In the Garden.* Mechanicsburg, Penn.: Stackpole Books, 1994.

"The Perfect Amaryllis." *Horticulture,* December 2000.

Peters, Ruth Marie. "Amaryllis: From Seed to Flower." *The Home Garden,* December 1949.

———. "Spectacular Amaryllis." *Horticulture,* December 1970.

Phillippi, Todd R. "Amaryllis: They Keep Coming Back." *The Green Scene,* March 1989.

"Pictorial Gallery of IBS Journal Covers." http://www.bulbsociety.org

Poincelot, Raymond P. "Plant the Biggest Indoor Show-Off." *Organic Gardening and Farming,* December 1972.

Price, Molly. "A Real Winner Every Time." The *New York Times,* December 10, 1972.

Read, Veronica. "Blooming Bold." *The Garden,* October 1998.

———. "Developments in *Hippeasturm* Hypridization, 1799–1999." *Herbertia* 54, 1999.

Schultz, Peggie. *Amaryllis—and How to Grow Them.* New York: M. Barrows and Company, 1954.

———. "Your Indoor Garden." *The Floral Magazine,* December 1966.

Spencer, Benton. "Redhots, Candycanes & Peppermints: All-Season Amaryllis." *Plants Alive,* December 1975.

Tinaglia, Susan. "Amaryllis." *Houseplants & Porch Gardens,* October 1979.

Tournefort, Joseph Pitton de. *Eléments de Botanique. The Compleat Herbal or the Botanical Institutions of Monsieur Tournefort, Chief Botanist to the Late French King.* London: printed for R. Bonwicke, 1719–30.

Traub, Hamilton P. *The Amaryllis Manual.* New York: Macmillan, 1958.

Troffer, William. "The Giant Flower in the Little Pot." *Plants Alive,* November 1976.

Turley, Robert. "The International Bulb Society: Our History." http://www.bulbsociety.org

The Visual Dictionary of Plants. New York: Dorling Kindersley, 1992.

Walker, Katherine B. "Amaryllis: A Miracle Unfolds." *Park's Floral Magazine,* December 1964.

Ward, Bobby J. *A Contemplation upon Flowers: Garden Myths and Literature.* Portland, Ore.: Timber Press, 1999.

Weston, T. A. "Untangling Amaryllis Names." *Horticulture,* November 1945.

Whiteside, Katherine. *Forcing, Etc.* New York: Workman Publishing, 1999.

ACKNOWLEDGMENTS

I am deeply grateful to:

Dr. Alan W. Meerow, research geneticist, systematist, and curator, USDA-ARS-SHRS, National Germplasm Repository, for carefully and thoughtfully reading my manuscript.

Katherine Powis, librarian, the Horticultural Society of New York; and Susan Fraser, head, Information Services, Marie Long, reference librarian, John Read, librarian, and Stephen Sinon, reference librarian, the LuEsther T. Mertz Library at the New York Botanical Garden, for their invaluable assistance in guiding me to historical and contemporary research materials.

Jackie Kallunki, assistant director, and Sarah Humkins, collections manager, the Herbarium, New York Botanical Garden, for finding pressed *Hippeastrum* species and expediting my photographing them.

W. Graham Arader III and Dennis W. Hrehowsik, W. Graham Arader III Galleries; and Evelyn L. Kraus, Stephen Donahue, and Susan Frei Nathan, Ursus Books and Prints, for locating prints and paintings of the amaryllis and for generously granting me permission to photograph them.

Mary Lineberger, rights and reproductions coordinator, and Mary Suzor, chief registrar, the Cleveland Museum of Art, for facilitating the use of the Charles Demuth painting from the museum's collection.

Jo-anne Ohms, John Scheepers, Inc., and Van Engelen, Inc.; Debbie Van Bourgondien, K. Van Bourgondien & Sons; Bill Whitlow, Amaryllis Bulb Company; and Sally Ferguson, the Netherlands Flower Bulb Information Center, for devoting time to telephone interviews and for giving so willingly of their knowledge.

Charles Barnhoorn, Henk Biesbroek, Sondra L. Lebost, Dr. Dennis Stevenson, and Chris Verdegaal, for providing invaluable information.

Barbara Hogenson, my gracious agent, for her efficiency, enthusiasm, and continued support of my work.

The marvelous team at Clarkson Potter, who made this project such a pleasure: Pam Krauss, my tireless, committed editor and friend who refined my text; Marysarah Quinn and Jane Treuhaft, who provided superb and sensitive art direction; Joan Denman and Sibylle Kazeroid, who shepherded the book through production; and Lauren Shakely, editorial director, who believed the amaryllis deserved this book of its own.

Yolanda Cuomo, our designer, who considered my photographs and thoughts and with great style and imagination created this stunning book.

And at home, every day I cherish and salute:

Pamela Foglia, gentle lady, for her attentive, vigilant help in the greenhouse throughout our "winter of the amaryllis."

Cassie Sigler, superwoman, whose home-management talents smooth my work day.

Robin Oury, Aldryth Ockenga, John Ockenga, Thomas Molyneux, Jacob Molyneux, Zoe Ockenga, and Nicholas Ockenga, who make our small family circle so sweet a thing.

And finally, my love and gratitude to Donald Forst, my husband and gardening companion, who encourages me—and indulges me—each step of the way.